I Don't Wanna Be My Mother!

What boomer women need to know and do now to stay smokin' hot for another 25 years (or more) even if they've been told it can't be done

Barbara Morris, R.Ph.

This book is written as a source of information only. The information, ideas, and suggestions contained in this book by no means should be considered a substitute for the advice of a qualified medical professional, who should always be consulted before beginning any new diet, exercise, procedure, or other health program.

All efforts have been made to ensure the accuracy of the information contained in this book as of the date of publication. The author/ publisher expressly disclaims responsibility for any adverse effects arising from the use or application of the information, ideas, and suggestions contained herein.

All links were correct and active at the time of publication. I claim no responsibility for the validity or content of the Web sites included in this book.

You may not distribute this document in any way. You may not sell it or reprint any part of it without written consent from the author, except for the inclusion of brief quotations in a review.

This book contains material protected under international and federal copyright laws and treaties. Any unauthorized reprint or use of this publication is prohibited. Violators will be prosecuted.

Barbara M. Morris, R.Ph.
Box 937
Escondido, CA 92033-0937
author.office@gmail.com

ISBN: 1-4499-9597-7
ISBN-13: 9781449995973

Dedication

To women who want to be healthy, productive, ageless, and smokin' hot in their maturity while their peers who chose to age gracefully play bingo with old broads at the senior center.

Contents

A HEADS-UP 1

SO, YOU DON'T WANNA BE YOUR MOTHER? 5

WHAT YOU NEED TO KNOW NOW 17

What You Are Facing at Forty (or Sooner) 17

Meet Your Existence Manager and Your Pit Bull 23

It's Now or Never: Design Your Future Life.................... 26

What You See, You Will Get 29

PITFALLS—JUST TWO AND THEY ARE MAJOR 35

PITFALL NO. 1: AWARENESS OF
    CHRONOLOGICAL AGE 35

Liberation Chronology: Choose Tradition
    or Freedom 44

The Sound of Chronological Age:
    Destructive Self-Talk...................................... 47

The Color of Chronological Age: Gray,
    White, or Whatever 54

The Appearance of Chronological Age:
    Wrinkles Don't Lie.. 57

The Sting of Chronological Age:
    You Don't Exit Anymore 62

PITFALL NO. 2: RETIREMENT—THE PROMISED
LAND.. 67

"I Won't Need As Much Anymore" 70

It's Not What It's Cracked Up to Be 79

Life in LaLa Land 84

WHAT YOU NEED TO DO NOW **89**

This is More Important than Sex, Money,
    or Relationships... 89

Educate Yourself... 95

Be Aware: Medications Can Age You 97

The Mirror Lies, So Deal With Reality 101

Battling the Bulge.. 102

Beyond Planning for the Life You Want 107

Prepare for Another Reality...111

**ACCEPT AND VALUE YOUR MOTHER'S GIFTS TO
YOU** **113**

Make Her Your New Best Friend 113

YOU GOT WHAT IT TAKES! **121**

THE ULTIMATE PAYOFF **123**

Claim Your Prize—You Earned It.................................... 123

THE "RULES"—A REVIEW **129**

**MOVERS AND SHAKERS OVER SEVENTY—
YOU CAN BE ONE, TOO** **137**

About Barbara Morris

Barbara Morris is a pharmacist, writer, speaker, consultant, and publisher of the online Put Old on Hold Newsletter. Her books include *Put Old on Hold* and *No More Little Old Ladies*. In her eighth decade, she is rockin' 'n' rollin' at her perceived age of fifty, enjoying all the perks and benefits of living a healthy, productive, growth-oriented lifestyle.

Acknowledgement

Thanks to everyone who contributed to the development of the manuscript. In particular, thanks to my creative friend and colleague Mary Lloyd for suggesting the title for this book.

A HEADS-UP

Hi Girlfriend!

I'm Barbara Morris, your new best friend. Welcome!

Right at the get-go, you need to know that this is not another antiaging book written by someone who has yet to experience "old age." I am a chronologically old woman (current age eighty-one) who has learned how to stay youthful and live youthfully while my peers chose or allowed themselves to "age gracefully." If you are in good health, you have the capacity to do what I have done.

About aging gracefully: You may not be aware that "aging gracefully" is a lifestyle that facilitates decline. It is practiced by members of the Church for Advancement of Chronological Age (CACA). Bet you didn't know that. But that's okay. I'll tell you what you need to know to avoid becoming an "aging gracefully" CACA practitioner. (I wish to be respectful here. The acronym "CACA" should not be mistaken for the meaning of the slang word "caca." Amen?)

What really separates this book from any other you will read about managing the aging process is my take on the decline-oriented traditional retired lifestyle. It is a trap waiting to snare unsuspecting boomers like yourself into a way of life that will deprive you of your chance to fulfill your youthful declaration, "We will never get old." Nobody (except me, it seems) wants to talk about what appears to be the final taboo subject. Sex, religion, and intestinal gas are openly discussed without embarrassment or concern that someone may be offended, but nobody has the guts to warn boomer women that they will likely be ambushed by the traditional decline-oriented senior lifestyle. It's treated as a sacrosanct way of life and questioning its purpose or usefulness in today's world is like bad-mouthing mom and apple pie. Because of that lifestyle, many unaware boomer women who are smokin' hot babes morph into depressed old broads playing bingo at the senior center and they never saw it coming. (Using the term "old broads" is not being nasty—that's what many older women call themselves. They think it's cute. It's not. It's aging.)

What I tell you will cause you to either cheer or jeer. If you ignore my wisdom and jeer, you may well find yourself smack in the middle of a traditional decline-oriented retired lifestyle, and you will wonder how you got there. If that happens, don't call me crying for help. It will be too late. Your goose has been cooked. If you cheer, then you are one smart cookie. You will never be "old."

Before going further, please watch my video. It always helps to see and hear the person trying to tell you how to live your life. Go to your computer now and meet me: http://www.audioacrobat.com/playv/Wn mQhY3s

SO, YOU DON'T WANNA BE YOUR MOTHER?

Boomer girlfriend, I know you. I don't know you personally, of course, but I DO know you. I can say that with authority because at age eighty-one, I've been where you are right now. I know what you are thinking about because I thought about many of the same things at your age. Yes, times were dramatically different then, but many things in each of the mature decades of life are the same regardless of your generation—worry about kids, work, health, relationships, marriage, and finances. Concern about these bread-and-butter issues doesn't change over time. What *has* changed is a new awareness that it is possible to manage and modify the aging process. If you make intelligent decisions early on, you can get through your forties, fifties, sixties, and seventies, remain ageless, smokin' hot, and outrageously vital, look and feel fabulous, and be of value not just to yourself but to others. Dependence and decline are not inevitable.

If you follow tradition, eventually you will probably morph into a reincarnation of your mother and start living her lifestyle. In saying that, I want to assure you that this is not about disrespecting or denigrating your mother in any way. Undoubtedly, you love your mom, and you should. And you probably wouldn't mind looking like your mom, who may look younger than her years because many older women take care of themselves and use cosmetic procedures as much as younger women. But behind the purchased illusion of youth, many moms can't hide "old" attitudes, beliefs, and behaviors, often a result of living a traditional decline-oriented lifestyle.

Moms get "old" because they just let life happen. They get "old" while they "age gracefully." It's the traditional thing to do. It will happen to you, too, unless you learn to recognize how, when, and where decline happens, and how to stop or modify it.

There is an exciting reality you need to know about, and it's embodied in the words of Dr. John W. Rowe in his book *Successful Aging:*

> "The bottom line is very clear: with rare exceptions only about 30 percent of physical aging can be blamed on the genes...only about half of the changes in mental function with aging are genetic. This leaves substantial room for a healthy lifestyle to protect the mind and body. And better yet, as we grow older, genetics becomes *less* important, and environment be-

comes *more* important. The likelihood of being fat, having hypertension, high cholesterol and triglyceride levels, and the rate at which one's lung function declines with advancing age are, by and large, largely not inherited. The risks are due to environmental factors." [1]

In other words, 70 percent of your physical aging is in your hands; only about half of changes in mental function are genetic. That's pretty amazing and it is not pie in the sky. Use that information to make gutsy lifestyle decisions that will help you manage how you age.

It's possible to take control of your aging process in ways your mom may not have known about—ways that can help you live with more youthful vitality and freedom in your mature years. Please notice I said "mature years," not "senior years." Right now, get in the habit of thinking of yourself and referring to yourself as a mature woman as you continue to age, never as a "senior." The word "senior" is loaded with negative images and inferences that shape and influence your self-image and your lifestyle. There is nothing about the word that suggests or supports vitality, energy, or personal power. It's not going to be easy to avoid the senior designation because it's so firmly embedded in our language and our culture. It needs to be retired from a mature vocabulary once and for all. Just as you helped to lead a revolution with the declaration, "We will never get old," let the "I'll never be a senior" revolution start with you.

You can do it if you know what to do or not do. Let's look at your mind-set right now. Are you moving in the right direction? Here you are, pushing retirement age, still proclaiming your intention to stay young forever, and you are not kidding about it—and good for you! You will hike, ski, and run marathons until your buns turn blue. You will hit the road with your Harley. With youthful enthusiasm, you will meditate for peace, save the planet, and volunteer at homeless shelters. You won't have time to get old. Yes, you are moving in the right direction, but…

That's what you think now. That's what you intend now.

Alas, in pursuit of never being old, you will be so busy "doing" that you will miss what it really takes to fulfill your dream of eternal youth—or what comes close to it. Trust me, you will need a plan. You need to be armed and ready to do battle with decline that is nipping at your heels right now. Again, YOU NEED A POST RETIREMENT PLAN IF YOU WANT TO AVOID LIVING YOUR MOTHER'S LIFESTYLE. (Sorry for shouting, but I want to emphasize the importance of having a post retirement plan!)

Boomers insist they are different from previous generations. They say they are "transformational" and will change retirement as we know it. That's just not happening. The reality is that every generation is different until retirement, and then, eventually, most wind up in the traditional retired lifestyle.

Here's a hot flash:

"Britain's post-war baby **boomers,** associated throughout their lives with social change, **are failing to break new ground** in their approach to growing old."[2] (Emphasis added)

And here's an even hotter hot flash:

"Most boomers—70 per cent—regard age as unimportant in terms of their personal identity and...they felt younger than their actual age. **Boomers regard themselves as being more like their children and younger people than like their parents** and...see ageing as something that requires managing but is not overly problematic...while **69 per cent of people interviewed agreed that it was possible to plan for retirement, 71 per cent were themselves making either no plans or only limited ones."** [3] (Emphasis added)

If you are not a Brit, don't think this doesn't apply to you. It does. In the Western world (and probably everywhere in the world) the aging process is still dealt with as if we still believe the earth is flat. We talk a good game about how enlightened we have become about aging, but we are still "failing to break new ground." A good example is the taboo of an older woman with a younger man. In spite of the growing acceptance of "cougar" relationships, there is still serious eye rolling, tsk-tsking, scorn, and charges of cradle robbing leveled at women who dare to challenge tradition. The old advertising slogan, "You've come a long way, baby," still has a long way to go to reflect reality. But you can change that, right? Are you ready to lead the charge?

With retirement on your horizon, if you don't want to become your mother or live her conventional lifestyle, you can't wait until you are retired to plan for a new growth-oriented second life that will maintain your "hotness." You can't retire and think, "I'll take some time to smell the roses and then I'll develop a plan." It doesn't work that way. The scent of the "retirement roses" can become so intoxicating that you forget about planning for a growth-oriented lifestyle, and before you know it, you are into the traditional decline-oriented senior lifestyle. Taking time to smell the roses is important but should be part of a defined post retirement plan for how you want to live your life. (It is not the same as having a financial plan.) You need to know what you will do when you are done inhaling the intoxicating fragrance of doing nothing every day. *Plan, plan, plan before you get to retirement land.*

The first couple of years in traditional retirement are like a honeymoon. You finally get to do everything you ever dreamed of doing. Perhaps for the first time in years you actually feel better mentally and physically because the stress and responsibility of work are gone. The freedom of living life without structure is so heady you think it will last forever, but fantasy collides with reality when the thrill of the "retirement honeymoon" begins to dissipate. After one too many safaris or trips to Peru to study ancient ruins, money starts to run out. Then serious unanticipated health issues begin to surface. Facial lines and wrinkles deepen. A wee small voice filled with head-scratching disillusionment starts to ask, "Is this all there is?" There is definitely more to look forward to, and it's called traditional retirement, the embodiment of the "you are at the end of the line" lifestyle. It's not a place for healthy vital women, but many will end up there.

Don't be one of the 71 percent that fail to plan for the life you really want in your maturity. The woman you grow into and the lifestyle that you live is largely up to you, and not preordained by fate.

What I Am Going to Do for You

In the pages that follow, I will help you in the following ways:

I am going to cut through the crap, the false assumptions, the pitfalls, the lures, and, in general, all the erroneous stuff you believe about the aging process that aids and abets your becoming your mother and adopting her decline-oriented lifestyle.

I am going to reveal to you what you need to know to grow into the vital, ageless woman you want to become as you continue to mature. Some ideas are repeated more than once to make certain you don't miss anything. I'll start by briefly touching on the significance of lifestyle, appearance, and what goes on in your head.

Your Lifestyle...

Traditional retirement is synonymous with decline and death. I believe that with all my being. Not only is traditional retirement not ordained by God, it is an unconscionable waste to throw away a lifetime of wisdom and experience because you've reached an arbitrary retirement age. You can accomplish so much in your mature years with your accumulated smarts. You need to listen to those nagging thoughts about "I wish I could have been" or "I wish I could have done." It is not too late to live the life you think it is too late to have.

Yes, retirement is an entitlement, and as you approach your retirement, please don't start to repeat the mindless bumper sticker slogan "I've worked all of my life and I deserve my retirement." It's a little like saying, "I've lived all my life and I deserve my death." It doesn't make sense to say you've worked all your life because you are still alive and you have not worked all your life. True, after you've worked forty years or more, you may be worn out and ready to kick back and do nothing, but traditional retirement should not be a destination if you are healthy and if you want to remain smokin' hot as the years roll by.

Your Appearance...

Looking good in your mature years is the easy part of managing the aging process. With effort and planning, every healthy older woman has the capacity to look far better than she does. But who plans and who makes the effort? How many women do you know who are aware that their youth has been slipping away since age thirty? Probably not one in a million, because youth cons you into believing it's going to be around forever. Every day you look in the mirror and you look the same as the day before. What you see says you are doing just fine. The deceptive reflection in the mirror is the ultimate trap that prevents you from making an effort to keep what you have. But you can avoid that trap. When admiring what you see, have the awareness to say to yourself, "Wow! I look great—I'm going to do what I can to keep what I have." For most women, it doesn't happen that way, but *you* can make it happen.

You are at an age when it's "now or never." It's your last chance to grow into your maturity in the condition in which you want to spend the rest of your life.

If you do everything you can possibly do to keep your body in shape but, as time goes on, you are unhappy with the appearance of your face (or most any part of your body), you can hire someone to fix it. Cosmetic procedures have come a long way, and they are becoming more affordable. A TV ad currently running promises a facelift in an hour. Again, looking good is the easy part…

What Goes On In Your Head…

While maintaining your appearance is the easy part of managing the aging process, the tough part of aging is managing what goes on in your head and the lifestyle you choose to live. While you can pay someone to fix the exterior of your body, you can't hire someone to manage what goes on in your head. You can pay someone to help you think things through but ultimately, you have to make decisions. Only you can do that job. You have to decide that you are going to be in charge.

As a mature woman, one way you take control is by deciding how (or if) you will categorize or label yourself. Let's talk about the word "senior" again. (I will remind you about it again later.) This is extremely important. You are what you say you are. I do not and never will refer to myself as a "senior." It is an unnecessary reminder that death is near, and when included in everyday conversation it reinforces the power the word "senior" has over how you live and the choices you make, or fail to make. It negatively affects your mind and body in the same way the word "retirement" does. It invades your subconscious with images of decline that eventually shape your lifestyle, and even your appearance. I guarantee—when you start to think of yourself as a senior, you will start to dress and look like a senior. Just as teens have their look, traditional senior women have theirs. Mature smokin' hot women have a classy timeless style that defies identification of age or stage of life.

The word "senior" is a psychological barrier to continued growth and productivity. Always refer to yourself as a mature woman in a constant state of growth. I promise—it will make a huge difference in how you see yourself, how you live, and how well you hold on to youthful characteristics. You won't always be able to avoid the "senior" label, but when you are psychologically armed you can hear the word, even when applied to you, and not allow it to impact how you think or live.

There is a lot to talk about relative to controlling what goes on in your head and deciding how to live. More about that later. Let's move on to what you need to know now.

WHAT YOU NEED TO KNOW NOW

What You Are Facing at Forty (or Sooner)

As early as age forty, an accelerating number of media messages, subliminal and otherwise, start to suggest you are getting old and needy. You are probably so busy living your life that for the most part, you are not fully aware of the assaults directed at your lifestyle, mindset, and your pocketbook.

Take, for example, the retirement industry that has its "go get 'em" guns trained in your direction. Businesses and organizations that provide services and products (some needed, many not needed) to retirees are a huge part of the economy. As boomers continue to retire, more senior-oriented businesses will come into being. Not only will these enterprises continue to promote and cater to those in traditional retirement, they will actively solicit the business and participation of boomers and legitimize their entry into the traditional senior culture. This means that unless boomer women are very aware, they will find themselves gradually sucked into a traditional retirement mind-set and lifestyle.

Here are some of the lures and traps facing boomers about to retire:

- Salesmen will want to sell you an annuity so you can retire early and live a traditional senior lifestyle in style, with a focus on living life as a pastime.
- Real estate agents will want to sell you a villa in a retirement community so you can live the traditional retired lifestyle with your retired peers.
- Travel agents will want to sell you senior cruises so you can socialize with traditional retired seniors.
- Publications that focus on your stage of life (and keep you focused on that stage and do not help you grow) will try to sell you a subscription.
- Organizations that solicit boomer membership but in fact are senior oriented are waiting for you. AARP solicits membership at age fifty.
- Government-sponsored community senior centers with entry at age fifty or fifty-five try to lure boomers (who don't want to be considered seniors) with "hip" programs. Instead of yoga, which might appeal to older women, Zumba is offered to attract younger women into a senior environment.

So, what can you do? How do you deal with all the stuff coming at you from all directions that suggests you are getting old? One way is to pay attention to advertising because advertising is powerful and it sells. Look and listen for subliminal messages and lures that attack your resolve to stay youthful and live a youthful lifestyle. As you watch TV ads, analyze them and figure out how they are trying to get into your head and motivate you to change your behavior or thinking in ways that are not in harmony with your intention to stay youthful. Pay particular attention to TV ads for medications. Pharmaceutical industry ads use boomer women to sell a variety of drugs to treat old-age diseases or conditions, including peripheral artery disease (PAD), gastro esophageal reflux disease (GERD), restless legs syndrome (RLS), and chronic obstructive pulmonary disease (COPD). When you see women who look "just like me" hawking such products you cannot avoid seeing yourself as getting old. It's an assault on your youthful identity. Why aren't obviously old women used to pitch the products? For another example, if you have a painful arthritic knee and your heart skips a beat in anticipation of pain relief promised by a TV ad for a new medication, close your eyes to avoid watching enticing visuals of old folks happily dancing, and listen carefully to the litany of dangerous side effects being rattled off. You may decide you really don't need to try that miracle government approved medication that could possibly contribute to cognitive decline or create another serious health issue that will make you feel older than you do now. You, boomer girlfriend, are the target.

One particularly annoying ad shows a nice-looking older woman wearing a sweater, (in advertising, a sweater on an older woman means she is no longer hot), moving almost in slow motion, fussing with flowers in the garden. What is she selling? Mortuary services. Where is the older man selling mortuary services? Don't older men die? And how about the ad for those living alone with a pendant around their neck to call for help? It's always an older women who has fallen. Don't older men fall? Yes, older men do fall, and I suspect they fall even more frequently than women do. The reality is that older women are often tougher mentally and physically than older men. Showing an older woman in the role of needy victim sends a dual message—that it's okay for an older woman to be dependent and compromised, and that it represents reality for most older women. The message is false on both counts and needs to stop. Don't think for one minute that such propaganda doesn't negatively influence attitudes and behaviors of many boomer women.

Ads portray older men in positions of strength and authority: a doctor in a white lab coat, a successful lawyer in a three-piece suit. I will know that advertising has caught up with reality when I see a competent older woman in a white lab coat playing a doctor. (Yes, I know young women are portrayed as doctors in ads—but older women can be and are doctors, too.) I will know that things have changed when obviously smokin' hot older women are portrayed as CEOs of corporations and as powerful attorneys. I would love to see Gertrude Boyle, eighty-five-year-old chairman of the board of directors of Columbia Sportswear, in a commercial. It would elevate the status of competent, mature women not just in advertising but also in the real world.

If you allow cultural "you are getting old" or "you are incompetent" messages" to seep into your subconscious, you start to look for signs of your own decline. After enough offers to help you do things you could do for yourself, or hearing remarks that suggest you are not as capable as you used to be, you can begin to question your mental and physical competence. Worse, you unconsciously begin to accept that the messages may be true, at least to some extent. Negative cultural messages sneak up on you and burrow into your psyche, skewing your perception of reality. Stay aware and reject messages that don't apply to you.

"You are getting old" messages targeted directly at you personally can be the most painful. Remember that tacky birthday card your co-workers at the office gave to you that said you are over the hill, and everybody laughed? And you felt like crawling into a hole or smacking them in the mouth? Such messages are hurtful and they are not cute. It's psychological abuse. You have to challenge unwelcome comments, especially relating to your age or competence. Don't let bullies or insensitive clods get their jollies by tearing down your self-esteem. Don't let them get away unscathed. So what if they think you are "too thin-skinned." You've heard the expression, "Old age is not for sissies"? Don't be a sissy at any age. Be sassy. Be assertive. Speak up and challenge ageist comments.

Age Fifty and Beyond

At age fifty it's time to get ready for what's coming at age sixty. Increasingly, others will refer to you as a senior, but that should not irritate you if you have armed yourself psychologically to deal with "the word" early on. You also have to learn to deal with boomer friends who have accepted senior status. It is through them that you unintentionally begin to participate in traditional senior activities. For example, an older boomer friend invites you to a meeting of senior women who wear crazy hats and she assures you, "It's a ton of fun." Who would want to pass up a ton of fun? Will you have fun if you go with your friend? You could and probably would have fun, but you might also experience an initiation. This is how the initiation process works: you accept the invitation even though you know you might feel uncomfortable being with predominantly older women. You do have fun, and your friend will invite you again to the next meeting. You rationalize it wasn't "all that bad" the first time, so you accept the invitation to go again. You will become friends with a few of the ladies in the group— and why not? They are nice, welcoming women who know how to have a good time. They will introduce you to fun activities in other groups, and before you know it, you are one of the seniors who wear crazy hats and you will be having a ton of "old folks" fun at many senior gatherings. Years later when you are firmly ensconced in the traditional senior lifestyle, you will look back and wonder how you got to where you are.

With an aware mind-set, attending one of those senior gatherings would be a good reminder to keep doing what you are doing to hang on to what you have. Do not be distracted by the fun, however. Maintain an emotional detachment from what is happening—as if you are outside looking in. That keeps you in "observer" mode and prevents you from becoming a participant. This is a good rule of thumb to follow as you go through your mature years. Keep your eyes and ears open and evaluate what you see and hear before you accept or participate in any activity that could negatively influence your intention to stay smokin' hot.

At age fifty or earlier, you will also have to learn to deal with socially acceptable self-talk that contributes to aging. More about that later. For now, let's meet your existence manager and your resident pit bull. You probably didn't realize you had these entities playing a significant role in your life, and you need to know about them.

Meet Your Existence Manager and Your Pit Bull

Within each of us, two entities influence how we age. You are well aware of one of them—your survival instinct. I call it your inner or resident pit bull because, like a dog, your survival instinct is trainable to a greater degree than you might think. I have named my resident pit bull Rocky. He's a tough, slobbering, do-as-I-say beast. I've trained him so well that when I'm tempted to sit and watch TV after dinner, he snarls and tells me to get off my butt and get on the treadmill or I will balloon from a size 10 to a size 20 in short order. Rocky constantly reminds me that as I continue to age and my metabolism slows, more effort is required to keep what I have, and that's true for you, too. With Rocky's help I keep reminding myself that youth is a short-term loan and to keep as many long-term benefits of the loan as possible, I have to work at it consistently.

The other entity is your existence manager, whose job is to get you to the end of your life on its schedule, not yours. This invisible creature resides within you and takes over after youth starts to leave at about age thirty. Unfortunately, as youth starts to slip away, it does not tap you on the shoulder and warn you that it's leaving you with a replacement. You won't hear, "Hey, babe, I'm splitting. I've done as much for you as I can. I'm putting your existence manager in charge. If you are smart you will work your buns off to keep what I have given you." Your existence manager doesn't want you to keep what you have right now. It doesn't want you to work your buns off to keep what you have. It wants you to let go. It wants to block your ability to think about or plan for the future. It wants to diminish your self-control.

Here's a perfect example of how an existence manager tries to sabotage your intention to stay in shape: a mattress ad on TV shows a young woman in bed and the alarm goes off for an early workout at the gym. A sweet-looking older woman (existence manager) appears beside the bed and tells her that she should enjoy the comfort of the mattress and that the gym will be there tomorrow. The young woman obediently rolls over and goes back to sleep. How often has your existence manager "appeared" beside you and hijacked your intention to do what you know you should do to keep what you have?

Get to know your existence manager. Know what it looks like and give it a name. My existence manager is Jezebel, a conniving Southern belle right out of *Gone With the Wind*. If I'm debating about "should I or should I not walk," mint-julep-sipping temptress Jezebel coos into my consciousness, "Barbara, sweetie, you worked hard today. You deserve to sit." That's when Rocky charges in and shows me a vision of myself in a size 20 dress. I don't need more motivation than that to jump on the treadmill.

You have to be tough and determined to win the war against decline that can come with aging. You need an internal ally, and you have it in your resident pit bull that you can train to help you achieve the degree of agelessness that you desire.

All of this may sound hokey and maybe even wacky, but it's not. It works for me and will work for you. Get to know the entities that inhabit your mind and body and drive the choices you make about how you live. When you "hear" your existence manager trying to discourage your anti-aging efforts, silence her! When you "hear" your pit bull urging you to do what you know you must do to stay youthful and vital—listen and obey! By the way, please don't tell anyone you "hear voices"—know what I mean? That's a secret you don't reveal to anyone.

It's Now or Never: Design Your Future Life

It's human nature to be "now" oriented, to focus on what is happening in your life this minute, today, this week, this month, but not much beyond that. Because you don't want to think about the future, and because holding on to youthful attributes is not thought of as a "must do now" activity, you lose the most valued attributes of youth.

A midlife woman looks at an older woman who has aged traditionally, and it doesn't register with her that she is seeing an image of herself in the near future. She thinks that what she sees doesn't apply to her. She is satisfied she looks "young enough" and doesn't want to deal with thinking about old age. It's part of the human condition to be in denial about aging.

Knowing denial exists, you can take action to manage your aging process. You can live defiantly. Start by taking an inventory of your existing youthful attributes you would like to keep well into your older years. Everyone has different priorities. Look at old women and decide what it is about their "oldness" you would like to avoid. Then deliberately work to keep what you have. That's what I have done and continue to do, even at my advanced chronological age. When I see a woman, perhaps younger than I, with stooped shoulders, I automatically straighten up.

What can you do right now that will serve you well in your later years? Can you climb a flight of stairs without becoming out of breath? That seems like a simple thing to do, but statistics show[4] that many boomer women can't accomplish that vital task. Can you bend and touch your toes? I can because I do it every day. How briskly can you walk? Being able to move quickly is a youthful ability. If you are slowing down, get your legs in gear by regularly walking on a treadmill, around the mall before stores open, or maybe your neighborhood is safe enough to walk outside. Old people in generally good condition often shuffle along, not because of "old age" but because they don't train their body to keep moving at an energized pace. And remember, sometimes you just need to be able to get out of the way in a hurry, so be prepared to move quickly!

Here's a challenge. If you are determined to slow the ravages of time, get a full-body photo of yourself as you are today and another photo one year later. Put the photo you take of yourself today on your refrigerator door or bathroom mirror. Let's assume you decide to walk thirty minutes each day—and nothing more exotic than that. You want to keep it simple and doable. Or perhaps you buy a simple workout CD, and without fail you do the exercises at least three times a week. I guarantee that if you stick with your program, you will be amazed and pleasantly surprised at how much better you look and feel one year later. You will be one year older chronologically, but physically and mentally, you will be younger. I cannot begin to describe what an incredible "high" you will experience when you see the result of doing this for yourself. By the time a year is up, you will have established a routine that is so much a part of your life that you won't give it a second thought. If your existence manager attempts to sabotage your effort, it will be easy to ignore it. You won't be entertaining too many thoughts about "Should I walk today" or "Should I exercise today"—because not only will you look fabulous—you will feel powerful, energized, and inspired to maintain the kind of youthful lifestyle that will keep you smokin' hot. It does take a year to see this kind of awesome change, so stick with it. A year goes by before you know it.

Think about a silver dish or vase that tarnishes. You don't see the tarnish build up, do you? Youth disappears in the same way—imperceptibly. To the best of your ability, keep your youth "polished"—don't wait for it to tarnish because the shine is difficult or next to impossible to restore.

Boomers and those younger face something generations past didn't have to think about: a longer lifespan. If you want an above average life in the extra years you will probably have, you must plan and work to keep what you have now, mentally and physically. Think about this: in 1950, there were about twenty-three hundred centenarians. Today there are over forty thousand. By 2050 there will be close to a million people one hundred years of age or older. You could very well be a centenarian. What will your life be like if you do not plan now for your bonus years? True, life has a way of happening regardless of what you do. You certainly can't control everything, but you have more power over the aging process than you think.

What You See, You Will Get

You have heard the expression, "What you see is what you get," and that applies to how you see your future self in your mind.

In order to create the future you want, you must have a clear vision of what you want to be like and what you want your life to be like in twenty-five years. You must visualize how well you want to function, mentally and physically. Having a clear vision and making a commitment to making it come to life is essential because commitment will drive the choices you make about how you live your life.

By age ten, I knew that I never wanted to be old. It was something I felt to the core of my being and still feel. My motivation was my white-haired mother, who constantly complained that she didn't feel good, which led me to fear that she would die before I grew up. One day while flipping through the pages of a *Ladies Home Journal* magazine, I saw a picture of a pretty young woman that appealed to me, and I decided that's how I would always look. That picture is just as clear and sharp in my mind today as it was at age ten. Have I achieved my goal? No, I don't look exactly like the young woman, but it is so close it is startling.

When you have a strong, clear vision of what you want to achieve, there is an unavoidable tension between present reality and the compelling vision. The fact that your vision is not your present reality is intolerable to your subconscious, and it will do whatever it takes to help you overcome obstacles, open doors and show you paths to take that will result in fulfillment of your vision.

Every day when you wake up, play your vision at least once and again before you go to sleep. Take action every day to manifest your vision, no matter how slow your progress might seem. Doing something, no matter how small, is better than doing nothing. For example, if you can bend and not get beyond your knees, that's a start. If you bend and stretch every day eventually you will touch your toes, and you'll stay more youthfully strong and flexible.

Take everything one day at a time. Start where you are right now. Whatever you choose to do, do it consistently. However feeble your efforts seem to be, do what you can do to the best of your ability. Always act with the end (your vision) in mind.

It's easy for me to tell you to have a clear vision and that commitment is essential, but it also will be helpful for you to have a more detailed explanation of how the process works. Please read an article by Joyce Shafer, "Say Goodbye to New Year Resolutions."[5] It's about far more than New Year resolutions. It explains in detail what you need to know and do to develop your vision and make it work for you.

My youthful vision of how I wanted to be when I was "old" drove some crucial choices I made about how I lived my life. In my thirties, I was reading Prevention magazine when founder J. I. Rodale was in charge and the magazine was really about prevention. I was relying on the wisdom of nutritionist Adele Davis. Jack LaLanne had an exercise show on TV and I exercised along with him every day. Richard Hittleman, also on TV at the time, introduced me to the benefits of yoga.

I was eating a "strange" diet every day that included homemade yogurt, wheat germ, and brewer's yeast. I baked my own whole wheat bread. I started taking supplements when it was considered quackery and only weird health nuts took them. Supplements weren't as "exotic" as what is available today. For example, J. I. Rodale recommended simple things like dolomite and kelp, and for Vitamin C, rose hips was the supplement of choice. It wasn't easy to find supplements, either. "Health food" stores were rare. Mostly I ordered from advertisers in Prevention magazine.

Long story short—why did I take this path? Because I had a compelling vision that remained clear, constant and consistent. I understood that how I treated my body long term mattered. I knew what I wanted to achieve and I stuck with it throughout the years. The payoff has been phenomenal.

Recall the passage a few pages back from Dr. John W. Rowe's book, *Successful Aging,* and be inspired to do what is possible: [6]

> "The bottom line is very clear: with rare exceptions only about 30 percent of physical aging can be blamed on the genes…only about half of the changes in mental function with aging are genetic. This leaves substantial room for a healthy lifestyle to protect the mind and body. And better yet, as we grow older, genetics becomes *less* important, and environment becomes *more* important. The likelihood of being fat, having hypertension, high cholesterol and triglyceride levels, and the rate at which one's lung function declines with advancing age are, by and large, largely not inherited. The risks are due to environmental factors."

Boomer women who want to avoid becoming their mothers do what they have to do to give substance to their declaration, "We're never going to get old." Recall what I cited earlier about how few boomers have a life plan for retirement. Here's a relevant part of it again:

"While 69 per cent of people interviewed agreed that it was possible to plan for retirement, 71 per cent were themselves making either no plans or only limited ones." [7]

Don't be one of the 71 percent that fails to plan for the life you really want in your maturity. The kind of woman you grow into and the lifestyle that you create is largely up to you—not your genes, not the environment, and not a whim of the universe.

Now, let's tackle pitfalls. There are more than a few as you continue to mature. When you know what they are and how to maneuver around them, the aging process and hanging on to your youthful goodies are not quite so daunting.

PITFALLS—JUST TWO AND THEY ARE MAJOR

PITFALL NO. 1: AWARENESS OF CHRONOLOGICAL AGE

Awareness of chronological age and its importance in our culture is in overdrive. It's a powerful, tyrannical force that, if allowed, can run and ruin your life.

Older women have been conditioned to play "the numbers" game: You know how it goes: "How old do you think she is?" "How old do you think I am?" "No, I think she's older than that." "She doesn't look bad for her age." Numbers, numbers, and more numbers, and they don't mean a damn thing. Well, they shouldn't, but they do.

The impact of the power of awareness of chronological age doesn't have a major effect on how you live prior to what is culturally identified as middle age. After forty to fifty (or thereabouts), consciousness of the number of years lived starts to place a "straightjacket"

on relationships, thinking, lifestyles, and business decisions. There is increased focus on staying young or
maintaining the appearance of youth, but the reality is
that after age fifty in our society, youth is out and old
is in.

But why? For many reasons, and here's one of
them: At age fifty, long before they are even close to
seniorhood, boomers buy into the lure of segregated
"active adult" cocoons (i.e., golden ghettos) where they
live a cloistered lifestyle in which youth exists only as a
memory. You've seen the signs advertising new communities: "For Adults 50 or Better." Better than what?

Boomers join organizations that promise youthful activities and a sense of exclusiveness and privilege
but are actually traps that encourage decline-oriented,
age-based segregation. Boomers can also get into an
old mode by thinking their age entitles them to special
benefits. I recall a woman telling me she couldn't wait
until she was fifty so she could start asking for a senior
discount. What's wrong with that? What's wrong is that
it creates an entitlement mentality that unbalances the
psyche to where it becomes acceptable to think, "I deserve a discount because I am old." *Because I am old.*
Got it? You don't have to be old to be old. You can think
your way into it.

When you have been conditioned to accept that
you are "old" based on the number of years lived, it's
easy to give up trying to keep youthful attributes and
grudgingly accept what society and tradition say it

is time to accept. An example is the decision to "age gracefully." I have already cautioned you about it—but I'm going to harp on it again because it's important that you grasp its significance. It is a decline-oriented way of life supported and promoted by revered cultural icons and antiaging gurus who have yet to experience old age themselves—old buzzards (most "aging gracefully" zealots are men—surprise! surprise!) who don't have the testosterone to do what they should do to maintain vitality. Their promotion of their lifestyle lures women who could easily stay ageless far longer than they might imagine. I suspect that the aging-gracefully guys want to make certain they have a plentiful supply of old "nurses and/or purses" to take care of them in their dotage.

"Aging gracefully" is a synonym for "dying gracefully." Many women allow themselves to age gracefully, based only on their awareness of their chronological age, social acceptance of the aging gracefully lifestyle, and a lack of full awareness of the consequences of their decision. Aging gracefully is letting go, just letting life happen. It means giving up goals, dreams, productivity, and challenge. It's denying that you can have a vital future. It's placidly waiting for death. A hallmark of graceful aging is a subtle but rapid and relentless onset of typical signs of "oldness."

Many buy into aging gracefully as part of the human experience. After all, we are born to die regardless of how well we live. We take vitamins, eat right, exercise, and then we die anyway. So it makes sense to enjoy life as much as possible—to age gracefully. No, it doesn't make sense when you can age with defiance and passion that result in a level of youthful vitality and a quality of life that is off the charts. Nursing homes are full of women who chose or allowed themselves to "age gracefully." You don't have to join those ladies.

Cherishing What Old Age Offers...

Those who choose to age gracefully often choose to "cherish what aging offers." It's part of the same mind-set. A subscriber to my Put Old on Hold Newsletter[8] unsubscribed, explaining, "I'm more interested in cherishing what aging offers me, rather than denying it." It reminded me of an incident several years ago at a speaking engagement.

At that time, I gave a talk about how boomer and younger women can manage their aging process to develop maximum potential in their mature years. The meeting planner had assured me I would be speaking only to boomer women. During the question-and-answer session that followed my talk, an older woman stood up and in a very pained, irritated tone of voice asked, "Why can't we just accept getting old? Why do we try to stay young when we know that's impossible?"

I was upset that I had offended an older woman who was happy or at least accepted where she was in life. It reinforced my awareness that many women get to a point in their aging process where they don't want reminders of what might have been, or what had been, or what can never be again.

My friend Mary Lloyd, author of *Supercharged Retirement: Ditch the Rocking Chair, Trash the Remote, and Do What You Love,*[9] sums up the effect of the "aging gracefully" decision:

"The sad thing about it all is that if you do the traditional '"sit on your butt and just let things fall apart naturally"' strategy you use up vibrant years of your life. Then when you end up really frail, you die a lot later than you are ready to and you are one angry, unpleasant old prune while you are waiting for death to happen."

Amen to that!

Let's think about what aging offers that can be cherished. Memories? Most are probably good, but not all memories are pleasant, and more than a few are best forgotten. Memories—even good ones—can be painful. Relentless reflection on the memory of a child or loved one lost thirty years ago is self-punishment that serves no good purpose. Cherishing memories to excess is living in the past. Yes, remember the past, but don't dwell on it, because what the memories represent are gone. Now is the time to look forward to creating a new life with new, fulfilling experiences that will energize you and help you maintain your youthful vitality.

There is just one thing about aging that should be cherished, and that's the accumulation of a lifetime of wisdom. Unfortunately, many older women ignore their wisdom and replace it with a yearning for the past, or resentment over an unfulfilled life and what exists now. That needs to change. Use your accumulated wisdom as a catalyst to create the life you really want from here on out. It's not too late. Don't allow the past and awareness of current chronological age to hold hostage all that you can still have and still be as a vital mature woman.

When planning for the future, there is always the specter of "fate" and how it can destroy a dream. There is no question about it—in spite of the best-made plans, life can and will throw a monkey wrench right into the middle of a happy life. When that happens, apply your wisdom and rev up your innate toughness to deal with what has been dropped into your lap. Life is not fair, but it abounds with opportunity to overcome adversity.

No one is foolish enough to "deny aging." We know we get old chronologically, but not all of us will get old. If mental capacity remains intact, we never ever have to age gracefully or succumb to being "old" and accept all the negative baggage attached to the "old" word.

Culturally sanctioned "aging gracefully" needs to stop. Cherishing old age or aging and whatever it might offer has to stop. Managing the aging process requires effort and deliberate future planning to stay vital, healthy, productive, and independent. There is no other choice for mature women who want to live, and not just exist, and keep their smokin' hotness.

Many women have learned to live and age well and not just exist. If you watched my video, you can tell I've aged well. Be assured that I am not an anomaly. Many women my age are in far better shape than I am and they are doing far more with their lives than I am. (I will tell you about older "movers and shakers" later.) The sad thing is that these remarkable women are often in the "age closet." You generally don't know about them because they shun publicity; they don't want attention that focuses on their chronological age. They don't want to hear, "Isn't she wonderful for her age?" or "Doesn't she look great for her age?" or "How does she do it at her age?"

Expressions of amazement for mature competence are patronizing and condescending. Ability should be valued and judged without reference to chronological age. My colleague Dr. Helen Harkness has a very successful career counseling business. She is the author of *Don't Stop the Career Clock*[10]—a book I refer to so often it's falling apart. She is one of those "in the age closet" women living life to the fullest, and the reasons she can do it are that she ignores her chronological age and, by not revealing her age, she doesn't give others the opportunity to make an issue of her age. Not knowing her age is a good thing. It forces me and others to respect her accomplishments without shading that respect with an awareness of the number of years she has lived.

Another numbers game older women are good at playing is called "You tell me your age and I'll tell you mine." Let's say you meet a woman at an event and she volunteers her age, expecting that you will tell yours. You could reply, "I'm ageless, and it appears you are, too," but that just raises hackles. It labels you a bitch because it denies the woman an opportunity to evaluate how well she is doing compared to another women she assumes is about the same age. By the way, you have probably noticed that young women don't offer to tell their age because their youth is evident and irrelevant to them. Only older insecure women do it.

Older women often tell their age, hoping, perhaps unconsciously, for a compliment. In response to the woman who volunteers her age in expectation you will tell yours you probably say, "Wow, you look great for your age." Then you think, "What a bow-wow. I can't believe those bags under her eyes. She looks a lot older than I do." If you are a nice person and it is obvious the woman wanting to know your age is in need of a compliment, tell her what you think she needs to hear. It will make her day and bolster her self-esteem. She will feel better and you will look better after you see the smile on her face. Being nice is its own reward.

About telling your age: when others know your exact age, you expose yourself to their biases, perceptions, and expectations for how someone "your age" should conform to their stereotypical ideas. Knowledge of your age influences how they will interact with you, and it's not always as you would like. The subtleties of ageist treatment are usually not visible to others but you know it when you are the recipient. It can be painful. Better to keep them guessing—don't offer to tell your age.

Is it ever okay to tell your age? It depends. Much older women swim competitively, run in marathons, or lift weights, and it's inspiring when we know their age. They put themselves "out there" for admiration and probably enjoy hearing, "Aren't you wonderful for your age." When revealing your age is done to inspire other women, it is a good thing. It's not a good thing when it's done to make other women feel envious or inadequate. Use good judgment. As a rule, it is better when age is not known. Mystery can be a good thing.

Here is something else to think about—every time you verbalize your age, you deepen your awareness of the number of years you have lived and the number of years you probably have left. Custom and tradition would have you believe that once you get to a certain age or stage of life, opportunities are gone. Let's say you are forty-five and you would really like to start your own business. A lot of self-doubt and negative mental discussion can go on in your head and be made worse by cautionary advice from friends and family. You start to think of all the reasons you are crazy to start a business "at your age." You rationalize that you may not live long enough to reap the fruit of your efforts. Recall that Harlan Sanders began his KFC fried chicken empire at an age when his peers were in nursing homes. Do you think he was thinking about how long he might live? I think not.

Bottom line: Don't advertise your age; don't ask another woman to reveal her age, and to the extent possible, ignore your chronological age. Refuse to age gracefully. The payoff is that you stay in control of your aging process to a degree that conventional wisdom says is impossible. It's not impossible. You can do it. You *can* tame the power of awareness of chronological age that would make you old before you are old.

Liberation Chronology: Choose Tradition or Freedom

One of the best ways to neutralize the tyranny of chronological age is to refuse to categorize yourself in a way that puts you into a "stage cage." Start by adopting the new stages of aging developed by Dr. Helen Harkness, based on the reality that our lifespan has increased by thirty years in the past century. She offers a realistic and workable guide in her groundbreaking book *Don't Stop the Career Clock*.[11] On page 79, she advises, "If we need some kind of aging chronology I suggest we design our own." The following is her "live long, die fast" contemporary model for aging:

- young adulthood: twenty to forty
- first midlife: forty to sixty
- second midlife: sixty to eighty
- young-old: eighty to ninety
- elderly: ninety and above
- old-old: two to three years to live

The above chronology makes sense not just because we are living longer, but also because we are healthier than past generations. It's become a cliché that today's forty is yesterday's sixty, but it's true. So why do we put up with traditional thinking and behaviors and classifications that limit potential and are as archaic as the "earth is flat" theory? You don't have to wait for the Harkness chronology to become mainstream. Exercise your individuality and adopt it right now. If you are fifty, you won't think of yourself as middle aged. You are simply in your first midlife. If you are sixty, you aren't elderly (as society currently labels you); you're simply in your second midlife. Adopting this chronology makes a huge difference in how you see yourself, how you embrace your potential, and how you live your life. It validates the youthful person you are regardless of your chronological age. It enables you to live your perceived age—the age you feel you are. It's truly liberating. Best of all, it destroys the power of awareness of chronological age.

I think perceived age should be a legal choice. Ridiculous? A California antidiscrimination law[12] allows students and school staff to define their own gender, meaning their perceived identity, appearance, or behavior. If it is legal to determine one's perceived identity, why not legalize the right to decide one's perceived age? Yes, I know it would create all sorts of legal complications, but I believe that if we wanted to, we could make it work. Laws far more head-scratching than legalized perceived age have been enacted and we have learned to live with them. Look, if you are seventy and feel and function as a fifty-year-old, why should you be held back in any way by anachronistic tradition?

Please pause and think long and hard about the following:

If you are healthy and if you could live without awareness of your chronological age, how would your life be different—how would you be different? (The question is not "how old would you be?") Would you want to "age gracefully" or "cherish" old age? Or would you live with joyful anticipation and have exciting plans for your future? Without question, you would be different if you didn't know your age, and not only would your life be different, you wouldn't have to put up with outdated tradition and conventional wisdom about age getting in your way of living how you want to live. Well, you do know your chronological age, but you can ignore it and live as if you will live forever. You will have given yourself power to experience a level of freedom and vitality only enjoyed by the chronologically young.

The Sound of Chronological Age: Destructive Self-Talk

I am certain you are aware that it's socially acceptable for a forty-plus woman to make deprecating comments about her age or abilities, but it's not charming, adorable, or endearing. It needs to stop.

Negative self-talk about yourself or your abilities is destructive. If you really understood how it hastens decline, you wouldn't indulge in it. When I hear a woman do it, I automatically assume the persona of Judge Judy at her crankiest. I am not above chastising a perfect stranger (with a smile, of course) for assaulting my ears with the utterance of one of what I call the "Deadly Sins of Negative Self-Talk." They are "articles of faith" of the Church for Advancement of Chronological Age (also known simply as CACA). Not surprisingly, CACA has a huge following of believers and practitioners.

You know what the sins are, and you are probably guilty of unintentionally committing one or more of them. Here are a few straight out of the Book of CACA:

- I must be getting old
- I'm too old to be doing that
- I'm too old to learn that
- I'm just an old broad
- I'm having a senior moment

Let's look at each of above CACA sins:

•   I must be getting old

How often do you say, "I must be getting old," when you drop something or do something klutzy? It's devastating—not that you dropped something but that you chastise yourself for doing what everybody does, regardless of age. Please don't beat up on yourself for exhibiting human frailty.

The subconscious is so powerful and obedient, and it can't differentiate between fact and fiction. It listens and acts upon what you think and tell yourself. When you mindlessly babble, "I must be getting old," your subconscious takes it as an order—that getting old is something you must achieve, and it will help you get what it perceives you want. Remember, you are what you say you are.

•   *I'm too old to be doing that*

If you have ever said, "I'm too old to do that," I will bet you said it not because you really believe you are too old, but because you think that's what you are supposed to say because you are at "that age." The wife of a friend I used to work with died suddenly. While working with him, he used to talk about all the "Walter Mitty" kinds of things he wanted to do, such as sailing, hang gliding, and other "daring" activities. He never did those things because his wife discouraged him—which was understandable because she was concerned for his safety. Sometime after her death, I received a note from him telling me what he had been doing. It included more than a few of the forbidden things he had always wanted to do. Then, in parentheses, he added, "I guess I should be acting my age." At fifty-two? I don't think so! I verbally smacked him on the side of the head a couple of times, and I suspect he will never again think he is too old to do whatever he wants to do and knows he can do.

•   *I'm too old to learn that*

I recently signed up to learn line dancing, and it quickly appeared that I may have two left feet. (Because I am "directionally challenged," I have to think about which way is "right" and which way if "left" which slowed my progress.) However, I quickly realized my feet and compromised sense of direction weren't the problem. While listening to the instructor explain and demonstrate what to do, I was writing an article in my head about how funny it was that I was trying to learn something that doesn't grab me in my gut. I couldn't wait to get home to get my article down on paper, and yes, I dropped out. I am now taking guitar lessons. My grandson Alex is my teacher, and he is determined that after I learn to play, or what passes for playing, we will let our hair grow long, get some ratty, dirty-looking rags to wear, hire an agent, and get some gigs as "Alex and Nana." It doesn't matter that neither one of us can carry a tune. We can scream very loud, and both of us can jump up and down which seems to be a require-ment for successful rockers. Originally, Alex wanted to call us "Bonnie and Clyde," and maybe we will. In any case, we WILL be successful because I'm not too old to learn what I want to learn, and because I'm in tip-top condition I can do whatever I want to do. And you can do whatever you want to do if you take care of yourself and plan early on for the kind of life you want when society says you are "too old to learn that."

• *I'm just an old broad*

When you meet someone and you are asked the mindless "How are you?" question, don't ever reply, "Oh, I'm okay for an old broad." Please, don't EVER refer to yourself as an "old broad" or use any other cutesy but demeaning "old broad" designation, such as "snappy old broad" or "sexy old broad." If you do, I'll call Judge Judy and have you committed to a retirement community where you can happily commiserate with real old broads who wear crazy hats, "do lunch," and fall asleep while the speaker tells them what they came to hear. "Old broad" is a disgraceful and disparaging term. Many years ago an article in the *San Diego Union Tribune* (October 24, 2000) reported about a two-hour TV film titled "These Old Broads,"[13] in which Elizabeth Taylor, Shirley MacLaine, and Debbie Reynolds mock themselves and their public image. It wasn't nice.

The article negatively portrayed Debbie Reynolds as the owner of a "pathetic hotel, where she displays her old costumes and sings in the casino." I've been in Debbie Reynolds' "pathetic hotel," and I can tell you what she has done with it is awesome. Ruined financially by several husbands, she bounced back to make a life for herself. She is an inspiration for all women regardless of age. Look, you can't stop others from calling you disparaging names behind your back, but you shouldn't do it to yourself, even in jest. Words are powerful. Love and respect yourself. You are what you say you are.

- ### *I'm having a senior moment*

My husband was reading the sports page and he started to laugh as he read aloud to me, "Can you believe it—San Diego Padre Gary Maddux fell off the mound while pitching and blamed it on having a senior moment!" Is Maddux an old geezer who should have retired a long time ago? Hardly. At the time Maddux was forty-one and, from my perspective, just a boy.

Telling yourself you are having a senior moment when you can't recall something, do something quickly, or do something perfectly isn't cute. It isn't an endearing unspoken recognition that "we are all getting old." It is aging.

It's damaging to say "I'm having a senior moment" because it is often said in such a prideful, giggly, self-deprecating way that it's akin to boasting that you enjoy it and own it. If you tell yourself often enough that you are having a senior moment, it becomes an acceptable, entrenched part of your thinking and eventually affects your ability to recall information. It takes a bit of patience and effort, but remembering is easier when you forgive yourself for human frailty. Whether you are a "senior" or a teen, rapid recall sometimes can be a challenge, and that's okay.

Another reason to avoid the "senior moment" drama is the word "senior" itself. I've already explained what's wrong with using the "senior" designation, but I want to be sure you to grasp the significance of the word. It is loaded with so much decline-oriented baggage you are not aware of. Your subconscious takes in everything from the culture that relates to and applies to the word and uses it to shape and influence your self esteem, thinking, behavior, lifestyle, and appearance. So the less often you refer to yourself as a senior, and the more often you reject the word as applying in any way to you, the more control you have over your aging process. Smokin' hot women are not "seniors" and they don't have "senior moments." They are not "old broads." They are mature women in a constant state of growth. Got it? Good.

I have never had a senior moment, and I never will, because I choose not to. Yes, I forget things, but I refuse to attribute fleeting memory lapses to "I'm having a senior moment." I have never heard a forgetful teen explain away a memory lapse with, "Oops, I'm having a teen moment." Youth doesn't sweat occasional memory lapses. Neither should you.

Carefully choose your spoken words and the unspoken words of your thoughts as they relate to how you perceive your stage of life. Words do matter. And words you use to describe yourself as you age, for better or worse, matter enormously.

If you have unintentionally joined the Church for Advancement of Chronological Age (CACA) and bought into the debilitating language and behavior it promotes, now is the time to call it quits. Now is the time to stop committing the Deadly Sins of Negative Self-Talk against yourself. You deserve better. Use growth-oriented words to describe yourself, how you live now, and will live in the future.

The Color of Chronological Age: Gray, White, or Whatever

Ignoring the power of chronological age is more difficult if your hair is gray, white, or in between. Some women look stunning and ageless with white hair. I am not one of them. What follows is my hair color saga as it relates to the perception of age.

Miss Dorothy, who cut and colored my hair for years, retired at age sixty—still just a kid. I was devastated. I miss many things about her, but most of all I miss her wisdom. For example, she said that she would rather be bald than have white hair. I really didn't understand the significance of that until I decided to let my hair go back to its natural white color. She grudgingly made the color change back to white during the last months she worked and, at the end, insisted on putting on some blonde color. "No one is going to call you a little old lady with this sexy color," she assured me.

I quickly let the blonde color go. Too much trouble to keep it up.

Big mistake.

No—a huge mistake.

Now, if your hair is gray, white, or something in between and you are happy with that—my blessings upon you. May you never suffer "white hair discrimination" or the suggestion that you are senile.

Here's the thing—no matter what your face and or body look like, white hair categorizes you in an instant. It tells the world you have lived more than a few years, even if you are young and your hair is prematurely white. Your white hair says you are an old person. There is no getting around it. You may be thinking, "So what. It is what is. Why try to hide it?"

Why try to hide it? Well, others, especially young people, treat you differently. It's not my imagination—it happens. It is subtle, and when you encounter it, you know it. It goes beyond the "looking old" issue—it relates to perception of ability and it isn't pleasant. "Old" people simply aren't considered as competent as young people. White hair says you are slower, not up on what's going on in the world, and besides, you are just *OLD* and our society does not much care for old people. You know that.

It's different with men. They can have white hair, no hair, a face full of overgrown grubby vegetation, look like a grizzled old goat, and it's okay. They don't look old. They look competent. They look distinguished. No, that's not true. They just look dirty. Yuck.

Here's what happened In the doctor's office that helps to explain how white hair merits "special" treatment. A young nurse gave instructions for taking care of my husband's minor surgery. She didn't explain it to him—since he looks older than I and has white hair, she probably assumed he was too senile to understand.

She spoke directly to me as if he didn't exist. What needed to be done wasn't difficult—clean the incision with antibacterial solution and apply antibiotic ointment daily. Then she said to me, "Do you need me to write that down?" Well, maybe some women would appreciate that, but I didn't. If my hair color had been different, would she have assumed that I had the ability to understand and remember her simple instructions?

Here's another example. A young woman asked if I had any great-grandkids. Excuse me? My grandchildren are barely teenagers. If my hair were a young color, would the question have been about grandkids instead of great-grandkids? Would she have asked about kids at all?

Long story short, I have found a replacement for the irreplaceable Miss Dorothy, and hopefully I will have enough sense not to let my new color grow out. I don't want to look like an old comic strip character you've probably never heard of called Gravel Gertie. She was a Hollywoodish old crone with long, scraggly white hair, and you'd be scared out of your wits if you met her in a dark alley. On the plus side, Gertie was tough. She didn't allow her advanced age or the color of her hair to get in the way of living how she wanted. And neither should you. But it makes sense to deal with reality when it comes to hair color. We live in a disgustingly ageist society that is all too eager to slap an "old" label on you because of your prematurely gray or white hair. You might not be offended if that happened to you; you might not mind. But I bet you'd change your mind after enough people asked you if you had GREAT-grandkids—at forty-something.

The Appearance of Chronological Age: Wrinkles Don't Lie

Every woman is concerned about wrinkles. We all get them eventually. However, they don't just show up out of thin air, and not all of them are genetic.

Let's get the argument that "you can't avoid wrinkles because they are in your genes" out of the way. Remember the passage given a few pages back from Dr. Rowe's book, *Successful Aging*:

> "The bottom line is very clear: with rare exceptions only about 30 percent of physical aging can be blamed on the genes...only about half of the changes in mental function with aging are genetic. This leaves substantial room for a healthy lifestyle to protect the mind and body. And better yet, as we grow older, genetics becomes *less* important, and environment becomes *more* important. The likelihood of being fat, having hypertension, high cholesterol and triglyceride levels, and the rate at which one's lung function declines with advancing age are, by and large, largely not inherited. The risks are due to environmental factors." [14]

It's easy to blame your genes for your wrinkles. But if you believe Dr. Rowe's claim that only 30 percent of how we age is genetic, you realize how much power you have to manage the appearance of your face.

The degree of facial wrinkling at age forty or fifty can be an indication of how you have lived so far. If, since your thirties, you drank to excess, did drugs, didn't get enough sleep, ate a crappy diet and didn't compensate with supplements, and have been holding grudges and living a lifestyle that you innately know is not healthy, it's going to show up on your face sooner rather than later. How often have you looked at a woman and thought, "She's lived a tough life," just based on the appearance of her face? Bottom line: the condition of your inside as well as your lifestyle eventually shows on your face.

While working as a pharmacist I had boomer customers who admitted to illegal drug use in their youth. They declared they hated drugs and regretted youthful drug abuse but they were still "doin' drugs"—legal prescription drugs.[15] They had simply traded a street drug addiction for prescription drug addiction. Their reason for taking prescription drugs was not to get high but to control pain, and they found doctors willing to provide them with what they needed to alleviate their pain. On one occasion, I called a doctor about prescribing what I considered an excessive amount of Vicodin for a patient, and he took offense. "Ms. Smith has severe fibromyalgia, and we are watching her closely," he explained. His tone was, "I know what I'm doing so mind your own business." Girlfriend, you can't be consistently "doin' drugs"—legal or otherwise—and expect to look and feel like a picture of health, especially in your older years. The face of a chronic drug user doesn't age well. It wrinkles prematurely.

So, how do you deal with wrinkles? The plain and simple truth is that in spite of billions of dollars spent on cosmetic products, there isn't a magic potion you can buy that will erase wrinkles. Yes, you can get good products that will temporarily hide them, but wrinkles are still there. If your wrinkles bother you, then here are your choices: continue to use makeup to improve your appearance, get a chemical peel or get your face lasered in a cosmetic surgeon's office.

How about Retin A? It won't remove deep wrinkles, but it does a fantastic job of improving texture. If your skin is relatively unwrinkled, but you have the typical "cross-hatched" appearance of older skin, Retin A will give you smooth, youthful-looking skin. I use it and love it. Caution: do not buy Retin A on the Internet—you don't know what you are really getting. Ask your doctor for a prescription and follow instructions for using it safely. There is a reason it's a prescription drug. One more thing about Retin A: it neutralizes vitamin D. I was shocked when a blood test showed I had a very low level of vitamin D even though I take a high daily dose of vitamin D3. If you use Retin A regularly, or take a supplement with a high amount of vitamin A, do yourself a favor and have your blood tested for your vitamin D level. A deficiency of vitamin D3 is responsible for a host of avoidable health problems.

I watch TV home shopping shows while I'm on the treadmill, and I am often amazed by the degree of chutzpah used to sell antiwrinkle creams. Before-and-after photos supposedly demonstrate improvement of wrinkled or sagging skin after application of the product, while at the same time the show host and product representative take turns oohing and aahing about what is supposed to be obvious and near miraculous change. More than once, I've jumped off the treadmill to get close to the TV screen to try to see the purported improvement, but I have never seen an "after" photo that I felt lived up to the hype. What baffles me is that the "miracle" product often is sold out. I don't get it. Why don't other women get it? Hope springs eternal.

In my opinion you can smear as much expensive antiwrinkle cream on your face as you like, but you will get far more benefit from a supernutritious diet and antioxidant supplements. For some time, neutraceutical companies have been promoting "beauty from within" vitamin and antioxidant products, but they're not catching on—yet. It appears women would still rather spend big bucks on temporary external fixes, which is unfortunate. Please look at "New Study Supports Antioxidant Supplements for Ageing Skin"[16] and see if it doesn't awaken your awareness that perhaps your diet needs improvement. Also read "Women Sacrifice Food Before Cosmetics,"[17] which claims that "women are not only reluctant to reduce their spending on cosmetics, but when their purses come under pressure they are more willing to scrimp and save on food."

For visual verification of the result of a nutritious diet, when you are in a bookstore look at Dr. Nicholas Perricone's book *The Perricone Prescription*. Before and after photos of women who have gone on his nutritional "28-Day Wrinkle Free Program" should prove that diet can be a powerful beauty treatment. No, you won't see disappearing wrinkles, but you will see how diet positively affects the appearance of your face. Some of the "after" photos will have you thinking, "Wow! If all it takes is eating right, I'm going to cut out the crap that's making me and my skin look old."

Does this mean you shouldn't spend money on antiaging creams? Not at all, but it does mean you should treat the inside of your body with at least the same degree of care that you treat the outside.

You have seen my video, and you can see my skin is in remarkable condition. I had my face lasered about ten years ago. To keep it in good condition, in addition to Retin A I use other cosmetic products that offer "hope." What I think is really responsible for the condition of my skin is that for years I have taken megadoses of calcium ascorbate, a nonacidic form of vitamin C which I am convinced has helped to keep my skin smooth and firm. What is a megadose? Between ten and thirty grams a day. The government-approved dose of vitamin C is about fifty milligrams a day. Isn't it toxic to take more than that? Well, after years and years of taking a megadose daily, I haven't developed kidney stones and I am still alive and in vibrant health. The body uses what it needs and excretes the rest. But isn't that wasteful? Maybe, but then, how do you know how much your body needs? If you smoke or have a medical condition or do work that stresses the body, vitamin C is quickly depleted. Who will you depend on to tell you how much is too much? Some things you just have to figure out for yourself. I believe the amount of calcium ascorbate I take every day, plus other supplements along with a consistently sensible diet, has paid off big time. Having said that, while it works for me it may not be right for you. Don't ever take something because someone else takes it. Do your own research first.

I am not going to get into the pros and cons of getting a face-lift. It's a very personal decision. When a face-lift turns out well, it can be life changing. When it doesn't turn out well it can also be life changing. I will suggest that if you decide to get facial surgery, do your homework before you decide on a surgeon and don't leave the country to get it done. I don't care how much money you think you will save. If it doesn't go well in a foreign country, what will you do? What will it cost to go back for repairs or touch-ups?

It's easy to say happiness is not about getting rid of wrinkles, that it's about loving who you are and living a life that is productive and of value to yourself as well as others. However, the reality is that wrinkled skin shouts "old," and if it bothers you, you really don't have to live with it.

The Sting of Chronological Age: You Don't Exit Anymore

If it is annoying to be treated as if your brains have turned to mush because of your white hair, wrinkled skin, and/or your chronological age, that's not the most irritating part of getting on in years. Every woman eventually has to face the "invisible woman syndrome." If that has happened to you at your tender age of forty or thereabouts, don't feel bad. Something interesting has happened in our society. The "invisible older woman syndrome" is affecting even young women.

How can that be? The truth is, men don't leer at women as openly as they once did because their testosterone-soaked psyches have become supersaturated. Exciting, nonstop female images have burned out their eyeballs, not to mention their brains.

How did the sensory overload happen? For one thing, women put their bodies totally "out there." Tight-fitting tops, tight shorts and jeans, and ultrashort hemlines are "normal." A display of cleavage is "de rigueur." Many female anchors on TV news programs look like they are dressed for a cocktail party instead of work. Augmented women abound and tend to look like cloned Barbie dolls. If you've seen one set of artificial melon-shaped breasts, you've seen them all. Mystery is outdated. What's to ogle anymore? (Please, girlfriend, don't jump up and down and shout obscenities at me. I'm just reporting my observations! If you want to wear skirts up to your wazoo, go for it. Just be sure to wear your panties. You might also want to read "How Much Skin Should We Show After 40?")[18]

Men get their fill of seeing naked or near-naked female bodies not just in everyday life, but on the Internet, in magazines, and with "easy come, easy go" hookups. They get all the sex they want or can endure. Aside from prostitution, what used to cost big bucks for the services of a foxy lady not too many years ago is now free. (Only older men remember that.) I think this is called "liberation."

I recall a stunning young woman passing by my prescription counter. At the same time, a nice-looking young man passed her from the opposite direction. He walked by as if he didn't see her. I thought surely he'd turn and look back after he passed her, but he didn't. Maybe he was gay. Maybe she wasn't his type. Maybe for a split second he wasn't thinking about sex.

So it's not just older women missing out on obvious appreciation.

If an older woman feels ignored, what can she do? If it absolutely kills her to be invisible, she can put together a determined, "you're gonna look at me or else" caricature of youth—big hair (if there isn't enough hair, an obvious wig will do), huge dangling earrings on stretched-out lobes, an exposed muffin-top midriff spilling out of tight low-rider jeans. A garishly made-up face plumped with so much filler it looks like a balloon ready to burst. It does indeed demand a second look, but it's pathetic. You haven't seen such a sight? You haven't been to Los Angeles.

Since you are a smokin' hot babe, I'll bet that you still get your share of va-va-va-voom glances. But be honest—what do some of the oglers look like? If they are midlife or older guys, are they clean-shaven or do they have a face full of vegetation that might harbor the remains of last Thanksgiving's turkey dinner? (Surely, you know that in general, men are not the cleanest of God's creatures. Do I hear an "Amen, sister"?) What do their teeth look like? Do the cave dwellers look like something you would like to kiss (or be kissed by) and be the recipient of a mouthful of bacteria? And how about a potbelly protruding out of pants belted at the groin? That's really sexy. On the other hand, if you hit the jackpot, lucky you! Chase him down the street and reel him in!

Most older women are rational. They do what they can do to look as good as they can, and eventually develop enough maturity not to care about catching the eye of eternally immature males. Wise women get to a place in life where contentment with who they are is more important and satisfying than receiving leering looks from boys barely out of diapers or midlife idiots who, in their head, fantasize that they still got it goin' on.

Love and value yourself and your life, and if you get an approving eye from some clod who fancies himself God's gift to women, you can pretend not to notice, look right past him, and ogle the young stud behind him. Younger guys are becoming more appreciative of smokin' mature beauty. That said, unless you are wealthy or a celebrity, it's more difficult for a gorgeous older woman to be considered relationship material for a younger man. I mentioned it earlier but it bears repeating: as enlightened as we claim to be, "cougar" relationships invite sneering, jeering, and raised eyebrows. I know there is always the question of a younger man's immaturity or lack of common interests, but if the age disparity is not that great, it's not a valid issue.

If you are looking for a long-term relationship don't allow tradition to sabotage your potential happiness by thinking a man has to be older. That's outdated horse-and-buggy stuff. Think ahead. Men generally don't age as well or hold up as well as women. That means when you are up in years, you don't want to be a caretaker; you want a "working partner" who can keep up with you. Please understand that I'm not suggesting nor do I condone inappropriate relationships with men young enough to be your son. If you feel the need to raise another child, adopt one, don't date one. Use your common sense and informed moral compass to guide your judgment.

PITFALL NO. 2: RETIREMENT—THE PROMISED LAND

If you are looking forward to traditional retirement, this is where you may decide we are no longer girlfriends. But maybe not. Maybe you will still love me when you understand why I think traditional retirement is an anachronism and needs to be challenged with something more useful and exciting that helps to keep you young, vital, and smokin' hot.

Most people look forward to retirement so they can finally hang it all up and "start living." Unfortunately, far too often the "start living" part of retirement doesn't materialize because the Grim Reaper unexpectedly shows up, or debilitating health issues surface so quickly that you wonder why you spent your life yearning for the time you would finally get to the Promised Land. The anticipated "living" part of retirement turns into merely "existing."

I think there should be an alternative to traditional retirement, and to that end, I am trying to encourage and legitimize a growth-oriented post retirement lifestyle based on balanced, lifelong productivity that has value for you and for others. It's a way of life that promotes and supports vitality, purpose, competence, and the ability to live life to the fullest. It recognizes the reality that we are made for work, and if we don't engage in work that has purpose we quickly decline.

I'll readily admit my vision of an alternative retirement lifestyle is not for everyone, and that's okay. However, many, many people retire not because they really want to, but because they are victims of downsizing (often a flimsy ageist ruse) or because retirement is the expected thing to do. They still have a fire in their belly but there is no support system—nothing that encourages or helps them opt into an alternative, productive, growth-oriented, socially sanctioned lifestyle that is accepted as a cool and enviable way to live. Imagine "the girls" getting together at McDonald's for coffee and, instead of reminiscing about the past and making plans to go the casino to gamble, they share what they are doing that is productive and adding value to their lives and the lives of others. Women who live useful lives look, feel, and behave differently than their totally retired sisters. Their vitality is evident in everything they do. They are the women who stay smokin' hot in their maturity.

Balanced lifelong growth and productivity create a way of life in which awareness of chronological age holds no power or influence. It supports a mind-set that helps you live as if you will live "forever." That mind-set does not recognize glass ceilings, brick walls, or forbidding "what ifs" or "it's too late" thinking that keeps you from doing whatever you want to do and are capable of doing. It is the ultimate antiaging magic. It is working for me and can work for you.

I do not advocate abolishing the traditional retired senior culture. I am not foolish enough to think I or anyone else can do that because retirement is an entitlement that is deeply rooted in our culture. However, I am hopeful I can convince healthy women that they can have so much more in their mature years than the prevailing retired senior lifestyle that is often not much more than a pleasant halfway house where you become feeble and wait to die.

Most people make many of their most important life decisions before they really know who they are or what they really want out of life. They spend their working lives doing work that is unfulfilling and they retire feeling angry, cheated, and ready to "enjoy" what's left of life, perhaps in a "misery loves company" retirement community populated with others in a similar state of mind. You don't have to leave this life unfulfilled. You are an intelligent, resourceful woman. Make good use of what you have discovered about yourself so far.

As a child your parents or teachers probably told you that you could be anything you wanted to be when you grew up. Conventional wisdom says you are done growing after you retire. I say you are not done growing. Now is the time to decide what you want to be "when you grow up" into your maturity. It can be as exciting and fulfilling as you make it. Think about what you have discovered to be your strongest talents and abilities. Think about what you could still do to fulfill your life and be of value to others. Dig down deep into your soul and pull up the strength needed to dare to be the woman you have always wanted to be and have the life you have always dreamed of. It is tragic to get to the end of life and find yourself thinking almost daily, "I wish I could have…" or "If only I had done…" Girlfriend, the best part of your life can be the rest of your life if you start to plan for it now. There is plenty of time left to do it, but it can't happen in a "play and decay" retirement lifestyle.

"I Won't Need As Much Anymore"

In his book *Age Power*, Ken Dychtwald, Ph.D., says, "Retirement is a relatively new and experimental life state that was initially envisioned to last three to five years, not twenty or thirty." He cautions that the current retirement model is not realistic for the future.

The future is now and Dr. Dychtwald is right. The current retirement model is not realistic. Our lifespan has increased by thirty years in the past century. Too many retirees are not financially prepared to cover the needs of a longer life. Researchers say that by age seventy-five, nearly a quarter of retirees will have experienced poverty, and the percentage rises as one ages.

As a pharmacist in a supermarket pharmacy in a middle-class neighborhood, I dealt with retirees every day, and what I saw confirmed they are not living in a land of plenty. With unlimited time on their hands, they cruised the aisles, hunched over their shopping carts, carefully looking for the best deals of the day. What they often chose were inexpensive, low-nutrition but filling edibles. Whatever they could find in the day-old section of the bakery and produce departments was a plus. Here is what's really sad—while they scrimped on food, they always had enough money for alcohol. They preferred wine and whiskey and bought a lot of it. Did they buy a bottle of inexpensive multivitamins? Supplements were not a necessity because the doctor assured them they are a waste of money if you eat a well-balanced diet. They were sure they ate a well-balanced diet. When you can leave the supermarket with a basket filled with "stuff," then you are eating a well-balanced diet, aren't you?

Should older people take supplements? In October 2003, a study funded by Wyeth Consumer Healthcare and conducted by the Lewin Group showed that daily ingestion of a multivitamin by older adults could lead to more than $1.6 billion in Medicare savings over the next five years.[19] Here we are more than five years later, with the government *threatening to take over health care because it is so costly, yet I am not aware that the government has gotten behind any preventive measures, and in particular I have seen no evidence that doctors are routinely suggesting to patients that they take a daily multivitamin.*

But hostility to supplementation is expected because doctors are only minimally trained in good nutrition practices, according to a survey published in The American Journal of Clinical Nutrition, [20] which examined the state of nutrition education in 106 medical schools. The respondents were asked whether current nutrition education was sufficient or if more was needed. It was found that less than one-half of the responding schools provided the minimum twenty-five hours or more recommended by the National Academy of Sciences in 1985. Seventeen schools required less than or equal to ten hours of nutrition instruction. Given this reality, it is shocking that many doctors, uninformed as they are, continue to scoff at supplementation when asked by patients for guidance.

Financial stress in retirement plagues the more affluent as well. As an example, let's look at my pharmacist friend burned out by long hours on his feet and demanding work conditions. After forty years or so on the job, he is eager to give up all the stress. Like most thoughtful would-be retirees, he thinks he has everything in order: savings and 401(k), Social Security benefits, and the traditional preretirement mind-set of "I'm going to cut back because I won't need as much anymore."

A year or so after retirement, there is an abrupt discovery that there is a need for more of everything, not less. He has discovered the benefits of working with a doctor who practices alternative medicine, but the doctor doesn't take insurance, so more money is needed for that.

There is finally time for travel and more entertainment, but the budget doesn't always allow it. Accustomed to preretirement unbridled spending and now having to think twice about expenses, resentment moves in as an unwelcome guest and refuses to leave.

What does anyone do in a financial crunch? Pinch pennies, use senior discounts, clip coupons, economize on essentials, play the lottery and hope to win a big jackpot, and take advantage of government assistance programs to try to make ends meet. A sense of resentment deepens, and when anticipated entitlements don't materialize there is bitterness and more resentment. It's not an ennobling way of life for anyone.

If pinching pennies is out of the question for my pharmacist friend, then perhaps it's time for him to go back to the old job. Maybe not. After just six months or a year in retirement, a lot has changed at the pharmacy—new computers, new programs, and a raft of new government regulations and company procedures. Who needs the stress? It may be easier to find less-challenging, lower-paying work. All of a sudden becoming a Wal-Mart greeter doesn't seem like such a bad idea.

Instead of retiring completely, had my pharmacist friend decided to work part time, even one or two days a week, he would have been in an entirely different financial situation. He would have had time to enjoy life and the benefits of continuing productivity.

According to a national study,[21] retirees who transition from full-time work into a temporary or part-time job experience fewer major diseases and are able to function better day-to-day than people who stop working altogether. That means it's smart to work at what you are doing now as long as you are mentally and physically able. Working part time will allow time to enjoy life, provide enough money to do what you want to do, help avoid depression, and keep you mentally sharp. Why relegate a lifetime of experience and wisdom to the scrap heap in the name of retirement? Why throw away your knowledge and experience that could be beneficial to others?

In the current depressed economy, things may get worse before they get better. I read article after article about boomers and younger people losing their jobs, and one thing that stands out is that they are looking for another job. They are relying on something or someone to offer them an opportunity. Maybe it's time to toughen up and decide what you would really like to do with the rest of your life that doesn't depend on working for someone else. Going out on your own is scary, but that may be the most reliable way to earn a living in the future.

Back in the "dark ages" of 1998, a Gallup Poll for the National Federation of Independent Business revealed that senior entrepreneurs (sixty and up) started or purchased two hundred thousand businesses. Over the years, the trend has grown, and it encourages ageless productivity for those wanting more out of their mature years than a rocking chair, pinching pennies, or endless rounds of golf, bridge, or mind-numbing TV. We are slowly making progress in the right direction. Self-employed people ages fifty-five to sixty-four grew by ninety-three thousand in 2009 and by two hundred thirteen thousand, among people sixty-five and older, according to the U.S. Bureau of Labor Statistics.

What kind of business would you like to start or buy, or what new career you would like to pursue? Are you a nurse who wants to own a coffee shop? Are you a physician who works for an HMO and wants to start your own business making house calls? Are you a secretary who wants to become a nurse? Then stop wasting time and start planning. If you still have a job and have been saving for retirement, continue to save even more aggressively, knowing you will use some of that money to help finance your dream project and second life. Constantly review, improve, and expand your plan.

When you consistently visualize your future in sharp detail, you are bound to reach your goal. Living your future in your head is energizing; it literally forces your plan to materialize.

Age sixty and beyond can be some of the most productive years of your life. Instead of incarceration in a nursing home or living a regimented lifestyle in a senior facility, you can and should be putting your accumulated knowledge and wisdom to good use. When you are healthy, working for others or having your own business can ensure a more youthful lifestyle that will keep you growing, energized, and connected. As a bonus, rather than being financially dependent on government, friends, neighbors, or your children, who have responsibilities of their own, you will have freedom and power traditionally enjoyed only by the young. You will feel like the cat that ate the canary, enjoyed every morsel of the bird, and anticipate the next appetizing opportunity. In short, you will still be growing and prospering.

The prevailing attitude about aging is that you will get old and decrepit in spite of what you do to try to prevent it, so why even think about a new career after sixty-five? To put current beliefs about aging into perspective, recall a time in history when the most respected scientific minds in the universe decreed the earth was flat, and everyone believed it until someone with vision and determination sailed off into the horizon and did not fall into a black, bottomless abyss. I have sailed off into the horizon of old age and beyond the horizon. From personal experience, I can tell you that you can have an incredible second life overflowing with unlimited freedom, choices, power, and opportunities. It's available to everyone with foresight and the courage to have more than what conventional wisdom says is possible or preferable at an advanced age. You need money to do it well, so prepare financially to the best of your ability.

The Meaning of Retirement

Ernest Hemingway called "retirement" the most depressing word in the English language. He is also quoted as saying it's the "ugliest" word. I think it's the most toxic word in the English language.

The act of entering retirement is loaded with conflicting emotions that result in major changes in every cell of your body—your brain, your vital organs, your hormones, muscles, and your life force—everything. It affects your appearance and your overall aura of vitality. How you see yourself in your mind's eye in your retirement is pivotal. Your vision of your retirement will determine if you stay hot or not. If your vision of retirement is laid-back, "low-energy traditional," your life force will slow and your appearance will reflect traditional aging. In response to your traditional retirement intention, you will create a lifestyle that reflects and supports that vision. If your retirement vision and intention are dynamic and growth oriented, your life force will maintain at a high, youthful level of energy that will show in your appearance, competence, and general demeanor. You will create a lifestyle that reflects and supports that dynamic vision. Everything in your body will work more youthfully and efficiently for a longer period if you do not internalize traditional retirement as your state of being.

Retirement has another serious consequence. It is closure on a lifetime of effort into which you poured your heart and soul. In the excitement of starting a new phase of life that promises freedom and leisure, few people think, except perhaps for a fleeting maudlin moment, about possible undesirable consequences of closing the door on the past.

The last day on the job, you are a "somebody"— a manager, a doctor, lawyer, secretary, or accountant. The next day, your life of contribution is over. You are a retired "has-been," now referred to as "didn't she used to be…" All of a sudden, public acknowledgement of what you have been most of your adult life has vanished. It doesn't happen all at once, of course; the process of becoming a "used to be" takes time. You don't feel the impact until you are faced with the first "Didn't you used to be?" question. Well, yes, you "used to be" whatever—but you are still what you"used to be." Because I am not currently working as a pharmacist I have been referred to as a "former pharmacist," but that's not my reality. I still am what I "used to be." I stay current with continuing education to maintain my license. You see, that's what the *perception* of retirement can do—it can try to rob you of a huge part of your identity. If you are not prepared for an unintentional verbal assault on your identity and capacity, it can result in an overwhelming loss of self-worth that is a prescription for the onset of depression. Unfortunately, the depression is often misdiagnosed or glossed over as, "you're getting on in years and you have to expect these things."

Too much unproductive time, not enough money, loss of self-esteem, rapid mental and physical decline—by any standard, that is not happiness, and it's called "retirement."

It's Not What It's Cracked Up to Be

I've already mentioned I worked full time until age seventy-six as a pharmacist in a busy pharmacy with a large senior clientele. I loved it and would still be working but for a family situation that required me to take off too much time and still expect to have a job. However, as I've already mentioned, by no means am I retired. I have moved on to other productive activities—writing and helping midlife and younger women reach their potential. I have also discovered a talent for Web site development. I can't think of too many things more mentally stimulating and challenging than learning and dealing with computer code and the beautiful things that can be created with it.

My decision to keep growing, stay productive, and avoid the retired senior culture is the key to the successful management of my aging process and is the key to your ability to grow into the woman you want to be in your maturity, not the woman you become because you blindly follow tradition and custom. Your mother may have done it, but you don't have to, unless you choose to.

Realizing life is finite and that at some point I might not be able to work, when I got into my early seventies, at work I began to pay close attention to the lifestyle and mind-set of my senior customers. I soon realized there was a huge difference between retired senior women and older women who continued to work. The productive women looked, dressed, spoke, and carried themselves differently. They were easier to deal with, perhaps because they were busy and had varied interests.

Just as patients tell doctors everything, my customers shared a lot with me about the joys, trials, and tribulations of being retired. I came to think of my job as my laboratory where I watched, listened, and learned as much as I could about the retired lifestyle. Based upon what I heard and observed, I got to a point where I found myself often saying, "There but for the grace of God go I." I knew without a doubt I did not want to retire or in any way opt into the traditional retired lifestyle because clearly, to me, it was not what it is cracked up to be. I will always be grateful that I had a privileged in-depth look into the senior lifestyle, thinking, and behaviors. Every midlife woman contemplating retirement should have such an eye-opening education.

What I heard and saw indicated that many seniors were content with their lifestyle. They went on cruises, played golf, worked in the garden, and did what traditional retirees generally do. They were happy and satisfied with life. I want to emphasize that this way of life is to be respected for those who deliberately choose it.

By far, more seniors were not content. You might think I heard a lot of complaints about health issues, but that wasn't the case. They more or less accepted their infirmities as their lot in life. For symptoms not helped by medication (which many seniors took a lot of), they relied on alcohol to help them feel better. Alcohol and medications can create a potentially dangerous cocktail, which they understood, but they didn't seem worried about consequences. One woman claimed to be in love with a guy named Jack Daniels because he made her feel so good and she didn't care about anything else. "He's better than senior sex, and I'll never get pregnant or a disease," she laughed.

I listened to tales of loneliness, boredom, financial woes, and a yearning for a time when they looked and felt better and had a purpose in life. Often it was heartbreaking. I recall a woman who showed me pictures of herself playing tennis when she was many years younger. There was an unmistakable wistfulness in her eyes and in her voice as she said she wished she could still play tennis. "Why did you stop playing?" I asked. "Oh, I don't know," she said sadly, "I just stopped. There were always other things that seemed more important to do at the time. You know, when you are young and full of energy, you think you are going to be that way forever and that you can always do what you want to do tomorrow. Well, for me, playing tennis tomorrow never came. Now I'm so out of shape there is no way I could do it."

I listened to stories of lonely widowed women vying for the attention of men in their retirement community or at the local senior center. Why any woman would want the old geezers (I knew who they were and the condition they were in) was beyond me, but when you feel alone and need human contact, I guess any warm body is better than none at all.

I heard bickering couples unhappy with each other; he complaining about not enough money or not enough sex (even though impotent and not helped by Viagra) and she dissatisfied that they never went anywhere and feeling put upon for oral sex too often.

Then there was the boredom that often resulted in feelings of despair. I can't begin to count the number of times women younger than I would say, "Barbara, don't ever get old. It's the pits." This lament was particularly common among women who had responsible, challenging jobs prior to retirement. They never quite adjusted to loss of mental stimulation. Some women learn to compensate, but unfortunately many do not.

The unhappiest seniors lived in age-segregated communities. They belonged to seniors' organizations and participated only in senior activities. One woman living in a government-subsidized "seniors only" complex was depressed about having to live with all the "old people" but didn't have resources to live elsewhere. "I'm so tired of the old farts complaining about their aches and pains and not having enough money. It's making me nuts," she grumbled.

For fun, many seniors went to casinos to gamble and get free or low-cost meals. Buses from casinos picked up seniors at community centers and other locations around town. That bothered me because many of the seniors could ill afford to waste money on gambling. I recall one woman at the pharmacy who objected to a small co-pay for her prescription because she said she needed the money to gamble. It also bothered me because I felt the casinos were exploiting the seniors. The casinos have more than enough money and don't need to take it from those on a limited income under the guise of providing entertainment. The casinos could have redeemed themselves if they had also used their buses to take seniors to classes that would help them be productive and earn some extra money for a better quality of life. That never happened to my knowledge.

Bottom line: you can't grow and develop when you are steeped in a lifestyle that is the antithesis of growth and independence. But you have free will. You can make choices early on that can result in a more rewarding way of life after you retire. You have to plan for the life you would prefer. It may not turn out the way you planned, but if you don't plan and you just let life happen, you will have no one to blame but yourself if you are not happy.

Life in LaLa Land

I haven't tried to hide my disdain for retirement communities. Created by savvy homebuilders who have figured out how to make big bucks corralling old people into walled and gated sanctuaries, they appeal to retirees who prefer peace, quiet, and an upscale place to spend the end of life. They are a lure for old people to play and decay.

Did I say they are places to decay? How can I say that! Retirement communities abound with things to do. Golf, basket weaving, hiking, swimming, bingo, dancing, scrapbooking, biking, and more golf. Even college courses for those who want to continue to learn. You name it—most retirement communities have every activity you could possibly ask for and perhaps even an unexpected "bonus." For example, The Villages in Florida would have you believe it's heaven on earth. What isn't mentioned in inviting TV ads is the existence of rampant sexually transmitted diseases in the community.[22] To be fair, given what's happening in the culture as a whole, one can only say, "So what else is new." I think retirement communities, no matter how upscale or activity-oriented, should have a black-box warning at the front gate: "Caution: enter at your own risk. This is a place where old people come to play and decay." I describe the lifestyle as living in LaLa Land.

In a new community that features active lifestyles, residents will be about your age. But what happens as time goes on? Assuming the community remains stable, there probably won't be too many younger people moving in over the years. You may consider that a bonus, but remember, over time, your closest friends and acquaintances will likely be those within the community, especially if your lifestyle becomes more settled or if you no longer drive. Imagine rarely getting out into the larger world or rarely hearing a young voice or seeing a young person. You may disagree, but I think that prospect is depressing. This is something to think about ahead of time.

Remember that our life span has increased by thirty years in the past century. Those bonus years represent a long time to live exclusively among old people where eventually, predominant topics of conversation will be about aches, pains, which neighbor is in the hospital or died last week, which widower is up for grabs, and what his favorite casserole is. It doesn't seem like a healthy environment in which to spend the end of life.

At one point, my husband and I lived for a brief time in a semi-LaLa Land. It wasn't gated the way communities are built today; it was a section of town with

semidetached homes for people over fifty. No kids allowed. Dogs were okay, but you would not have known
it by the reactions we got to our ten-pound (when soak-
ing wet) pooch when we took her for a walk.

We were conscientious about picking up after
her. One evening she took an unusually long time to
do her business, and when she finally decided to move
on, somewhere in the darkness a voice croaked, "Pick it
up!" There was nothing to pick up. Our little dear was
constipated. In frustration, I yelled back to the irritated
voice, "There is nothing to pick up! Come and show me
where it is!" Another time several women had stopped
to chat and as we approached them, our little darling
decided to pee-pee. One of the lovely ladies snarled,
"Your dog is staining the grass." I said "good evening"
and moved on. By the way, we were referred to as "that
couple that still works." I'm not sure if it was said in a
spirit of envy or disdain. I suspect it was the latter.

You might wonder why we moved into a senior
community in the first place. Well, we were "young and
foolish" (at fifty-something) and we wanted to live close
to the beach. We also thought that since we were working we wouldn't be spending a lot of time there, so it
didn't matter that neighbors were seniors. Long story
short, eventually we moved, older and wiser, realizing
that living by the beach was not all that important if
you have to live among cranky seniors.

To sum it up, for a healthy vibrant woman, traditional retirement should not be a destination of choice. If you choose to move to the Promised Land, you will decline faster than you can imagine. Don't think you can "try it out" and leave if you don't like it. The Promised Land is on a one-way street. There is a gate at the entry that swings one way—in. It does not revolve. Make the right choice. When your retired peers are "aging gracefully," you can still be rockin' and rollin' and smokin' hot, living a life you love.

Let's move on to learn about what you need to do now.

WHAT YOU NEED TO DO NOW

This is More Important than Sex, Money, or Relationships

What you need to do now is to focus on maintaining and improving your health. From midlife on, your health is your most important asset and possession. Your health is more important than money, sex, power, or relationships. Keeping and maintaining it must be a priority activity. With vibrant health, money is better, sex is fantastic, power is more awesome, and relationships are what you choose to make them. When your peers are incarcerated in nursing homes and you are still kicking up dust with your Harley, optimum health is the ultimate brass ring.

All healthy older women can age far better than they do. It just takes having a plan and working the plan early on—at least by age forty. I know it takes effort, and that goes against human nature, but you have to do it. It's easy to rationalize that you are going to die sooner or later, so why bother, but that's a trap. Recall that earlier I told you about your existence manager and your resident pit bull—the survival and anti-survival instincts that reside in everyone. Taking control of these entities gives you power to manage your life in such a way that the good health and youthful goodies you have right now can hang around far longer than is possible for most women. Remember, when you don't feel like doing whatever it is you know you should do to keep what you have, that's your existence manager trying to drag you to your finish line on its schedule, not yours.

While it does take effort, maintaining your health is not work; it's an exciting challenge and an opportunity to prove to yourself that you can be what you want to be and do what you want to do with your life, regardless of chronological age. When your health is what it should be, you can get to sixty, seventy, and beyond feeling like a kid, looking great, being your most productive, future oriented, and saying, "Wow! What a power trip! Why isn't everybody doing it?"

Not everybody is doing it because we want to enjoy life even if what we do in the name of enjoyment brings us down. Take food, for example. In our society, we deplore all kinds of abuses: drug abuse, alcohol abuse, tobacco abuse. We have all kinds of laws, regulations, and programs to stop or inhibit these abuses. Yet when it comes to food, not only do we abuse it, not only do we tolerate abusing it, we celebrate abusing it. Gluttony has become a new American religion, and for our worship of mindless ingestion, our rewards are obesity, diabetes, and premature aging.

Ninety percent of what's spent for food is spent on processed food that is unhealthy and aging. Tradition, custom, advertising, and impulse buying contribute to the problem. We talk about food with co-workers. We exchange recipes and subscribe to recipe magazines. We eat to relieve boredom, anxiety, and to facilitate social activities.

If you want to be in premium condition in your maturity, your relationship with food has to change. You need to get to a point where you choose to eat to live, rather than live to eat. You must become the master of what you put in your mouth. You don't have to become a martyr about food and feel deprived. You can learn to enjoy food that's good for you just as easily as you enjoy junk that's aging you. It will pay off at the time when you need it most.

You have to start somewhere to get a handle on what you put into your mouth. Below are some simple things to help you get started.

- Check your freezer. How many quarts of ice cream do you have? Is the fridge packed with sodas? Don't replace any of it. Diet soda as well as regular soda does more to sabotage weight management than you realize.[23] Ditch the soda and drink green and white tea instead. Get rid of sugar-laden, artificially colored drinks that are piling on the pounds. And while you are in the fridge, toss the leftover pizza from last week. Moldy food is not good for you.

- Don't allow your skin to look and feel like crinkly crepe paper. Drink more water to stay a juicy plum instead of becoming a dried prune. You need eight to ten glasses of water a day. As you get older, there is a tendency to lose the sense of thirst, so you need to drink water even when you don't feel thirsty. Keep a gallon bottle of unfluoridated water on the kitchen counter or at work. Drink at least half of it every day. Having it in plain sight will help you drink more of it. About fluoride: regardless of how many experts tell you that the small amount of fluoride added to the water supply is safe, bear in mind it's a poison. I have a filter at my kitchen sink that takes fluoride out of our drinking water. The amount ingested from municipal water builds up because of fluoride added to commonly used products such as mouthwash, toothpaste, dental floss, and even nail polish. How much poison is too much to consume safely?

- Check your pantry. Don't restock chips, cookies, toaster pastries, and sugary breakfast "cereals." It's just as quick and easy to scramble a couple of eggs or egg whites for breakfast as it is to wait for a pastry to heat in the toaster. What's faster than whipping up a protein drink in a blender?

• Having a whole foods market nearby makes it easy to cut down on processed food. If you make a trip a couple of times a week, you can get all the superfresh veggies and fruit you will need to provide a healthier diet for you and your family. For protein, try chicken—preferably baked or roasted. I use a lot of ground chicken—you can prepare it in so many ways. If you are pressed for time, many whole foods markets offer excellent takeout.

• Eat more fish—maybe. I rarely buy fish because it's so difficult to get good fish. I'd rather take fish oil capsules than eat supermarket fish that looks like it has seen better days, and probably has. Don't be fooled by pretty pink salmon. If raised in a fish farm, a chemical added to the artificial feed controls the color.

• Skip deep-fried anything. Since you won't need your deep fat fryer anymore, throw it away. (Well, okay, give it away. But you won't be doing anyone a favor.) If you must sauté, use olive oil.

• If you are an emotional eater, eat unbuttered popcorn or dry roasted nuts. How about an apple to keep your mouth busy? And who says you have to keep shoving something into your mouth while you watch TV? I know it's old-fashioned, but try knitting or embroidery to keep your hands busy. It won't make you fat.

- Make your own soft spread by mixing butter with an equal amount of olive oil.

- Give up complicated cooking. If your favorite recipe has a long list of ingredients, cut out calorie-laden ingredients that may not be necessary. If a recipe calls for a cup of sugar or a stick of butter—are you kidding? If you are buying a pound of sugar more often than once every couple of years, you are not doing your health a favor. Refined sugar is aging!

- Develop an allergy to TV food shows. They only whet your appetite to eat more and more of what packs on the pounds. I cringe when I see a chef plop a stick of butter into a frying pan as if it's nothing. It gives you permission to do the same thing in your kitchen.

- Don't treat food as your best friend or a mother substitute. Find nonfood ways to enjoy life and find comfort.

If you follow the suggestions above, and continue to educate yourself, "eating right" is a no-brainer. At this stage of your life, your body needs the extra tender loving care provided by a top-notch diet. I know the health problems you are dealing with now—arthritis, GERD, hearing and vision loss, diabetes, creaky hips and knees, to name a few. Without a doubt, what you put into your mouth from here on out will have a huge impact on how well you are able to manage what is ailing you today.

Being responsible for your health is more important than ever because it's not known what will happen with health care in the future. If there is rationing, a hip or knee replacement might not be allowed because of your age, so you need to be open to what is available now that is not traditional but potentially helpful. For example, if you are dealing with an arthritic knee, would you consider Platelet Rich Plasma (PRP) injections in your knee to try to rebuild cartilage and possibly avoid a replacement down the road? Would you take a type II collagen supplement to try to rebuild cartilage? It's a decision you would make only after educating yourself. The more you know, the more power and control you have over your health.

It's time to wean yourself off fast food and anything else that is destroying your health. Then decide how far you are willing to open your mind to alternative health care. Good health doesn't come out of a prescription bottle—I'll talk more about that later.

Educate Yourself

It's so easy to educate yourself. Bookstore shelves groan with books written by worthy physicians and nutritionists. Whole foods markets have a wide selection of magazines and books. Be careful about what you find on the Internet. While it can be a great resource for information, I don't think I'd trust a whole lot of what's out in cyberspace until after doing a lot of book reading. The more you read, the more you will realize that you still have a lot to learn, but you will be light years ahead of your peers who are still feasting on sodas and corn dogs.

You probably know more than enough about eating right but you don't put it into practice. However, you probably don't know enough about supplements. You need to learn about them because diet alone can't and won't keep you healthy. Part of your self-education should include collaboration with a naturopath or doctor who has had training in antiaging medicine, nutrition, and hormone management. If nothing else, subscribe to a newsletter that teaches about common-sense medicine and supplements. I like Dr. Julian Whitaker's "Health and Healing" newsletter.[24]

In your search for a properly trained physician, be wary. Doctors with limited knowledge about antiaging medicine and nutrition advertise as antiaging doctors because that's where the money is, meaning they don't take insurance. Their patients pay cash. A good antiaging physician or naturopath is a treasure, so search for one carefully. The sooner you partner with a good antiaging physician, the more success you will have managing your aging process. A good place to find one in your area is online at the American College for Advancement of Medicine Web site (www.AAM.org) or the American Association of Naturopathic Physicians (http://www.naturopathic.org/). If these sites don't list a doctor in your area and if there is an independent pharmacy near you, that is a good place to get a recommendation. Independent pharmacists are often sympathetic to antiaging medicine and know which doctors to recommend. Don't be afraid to shop around until you find a doctor who is in sync with your goals. They are businesspeople, not gods, so don't be afraid to deal with them as fellow human beings.

Be Aware: Medications Can Age You

Assuming you may be treated by a traditionally trained physician for some ailment, I'm going to touch briefly on medications as they relate to your ability to manage your aging process. Medication can help you live longer and better. On the other hand, many medications have adverse side effects that are worse than the symptoms being treated. If you have one or more medical conditions, it's in your best interest to know as much as possible about your ailment, but you also need to know about the medications used to manage your situation. You must become an informed participant in your health care and disease management. Please understand that your health is your responsibility. It is not your doctor's responsibility.

Many people believe that good health comes in a prescription bottle. One day at the pharmacy a customer was extolling the benefits of modern medicine, and I agreed until he said he thought it was wonderful that he could eat whatever he wanted because he could take a pill to "cure" his high cholesterol. There isn't a "cure" for high cholesterol.

High cholesterol is usually treated with "statin" drugs. These drugs effectively control cholesterol, but they can have some disturbing side effects. They are very hard on the liver and inhibit the formation of a substance called CoQ10, which is essential for the health of your heart and muscles throughout your body. Cognitive problems, muscle pain, and muscle deterioration are serious side effects of statin drugs and are more common than most people realize. I recall a man at the pharmacy who was taking a statin drug. One day he complained to me that he felt he was losing his memory. He had called his mother and called her again the next day with no memory of having called the day before. He also complained about muscle pain in his legs. He laughed about it and chalked it up to old age—at sixty-five. I gave him product information that confirmed the drug he was taking might cause cognitive problems or muscle pain. I also suggested that he read *Statin Drugs Side Effects and the Misguided War on Cholesterol* by Duane Graveline, M.D. He spoke to his doctor, and the doctor assured him everything was okay and he should continue to take his statin medication. What would you have done?

When your doctor prescribes anything for you, ask about potential side effects and potential interactions with medications you are currently taking. For a more complete picture of what you may be subjecting yourself to with medication, when you go to the pharmacy to get your prescription filled, ask for the package (product) insert for the medication. Most pharmacists will be happy to give it to you. You won't be able to understand a lot of it, but you will be able to understand the listed side effects and warnings. If you are concerned by what you read, don't hesitate to have a discussion with your doctor, citing the information you have in your hand. After you do that, it's up to you to decide if you want to take the medication or ask for a different medication. It's your right to decide not to take any medication. Don't be timid. It's your body and your life.

But there is even more you need to be aware of. Medication-induced nutrient loss is responsible for more health problems than anyone realizes. The pharmaceutical companies do not mention nutrient loss in advertising, although warnings may appear in literature no one reads. And chances are that traditionally trained physicians and pharmacists aren't educated enough about medication-induced nutrient loss.

For example, has your physician or pharmacist ever warned you that estrogen replacement depletes magnesium? Or that magnesium depletion causes muscle weakness, depression, dizziness, hypertension, and heart problems? That doesn't mean you should stop taking estrogen (if in fact you choose to replace estrogen), but you do need to make certain you are getting enough magnesium. A physician who practices integrative medicine (also called alternative or complementary medicine) will know enough to prescribe compensating nutrients.

Blood pressure medications such as Tenormin and Lopressor deplete CoQ10, which is vital to stabilize cellular membranes and give cells energy to function.

Diuretics ("water pills") may cause magnesium, potassium, and zinc depletion. Men with prostate problems already tend to have zinc deficiency, and if it is not supplemented, the prostate can enlarge.

Medications such as Tagamet and Pepcid cause depletion of vitamin B12 and folic acid. A deficiency of these two vitamins causes homocysteine levels to rise. High homocysteine causes irritation of blood vessel walls. When cholesterol flows throw them, it clings to the irritated walls, and then you have clogged arteries. We can't live without cholesterol. It is vital for cell membrane integrity and hormone production, among other things. But we can't live with cholesterol when it is clogging arteries as a result of high homocysteine. If your cholesterol is high, ask your doctor for a blood test that will determine your level of homocysteine as well as something else called "C reactive protein" or CRP.

If you want to learn more about how prescription medications deplete nutrients, read the *Drug-Induced Nutrient Depletion Handbook* by Ross Pelton, James B. Lavalle, and Ernest B. Hawkins.

Don't suffer premature aging and loss of youthful attributes due to dietary indiscretion, medications, neglect, or just not knowing. When you learn to compensate for dietary shortcomings with supplements, and find a doctor who can help you avoid what you don't need, or help with what you do need, you will stay healthier and more youthful a lot longer.

Once more: superior health and youthful longevity do not come out of a prescription bottle. If you must take medication, learn about the condition you have and understand the medication you are taking to manage it. Become an informed participant in your health care. Without vibrant health, your mature years suffer. You may not be able to do the things you want to do, which results in frustration and regret that you didn't take better care of yourself when you had the opportunity.

The Mirror Lies, So Deal With Reality

One of the toughest and most critically important things you need to do is to stay aware of and manage how your body is changing over time. Your body is the house you live in. Like the physical house you and your family occupy, the exterior of your body can be painted, patched, and remodeled. You can resize it with diet and exercise. As you age, don't think that no matter what you do a pudgy body is inevitable. You can be a shapely size 8 or 10 forever if you are willing to make a reasonable amount of effort. You don't have to be a gym rat or obsesses over it—it's really not that difficult. I'm doing it and you can do it, too.

I've mentioned it before but it bears repeating. It's difficult to manage physical change because every day the image you see in the mirror seems not to change, and as a result it lulls you into a false sense of "I'm doing just fine. I'm holding my own." Youth cons you into believing it will be around forever and that you don't have to ever pay a price to keep any of it. Youth conspires with the mirror to beguile you into inactivity. Don't fall for the ruse.

You are in charge of your aging process when you realize that the young or "okay" image you see and admire in the mirror isn't going to be there forever. That's when you decide that your youth, or at least as many youthful attributes as you can control, will not be allowed to slip away without a fight.

Battling the Bulge

Controlling weight is a major challenge. One of the best ways to fight weight gain is to refuse to buy a size larger when your clothes get too tight. If all of a sudden your jeans feel too snug, immediately take action to undo the snugness. No ifs, ands, or buts.

How do you do that? Surely you have a treadmill. If not, get one—it's your best friend to help control weight. If your jeans become snug when walking thirty minutes a day three times a week, then step up your routine to thirty minutes every day. If that doesn't do it, then look realistically at what and when you are eating. No time to exercise? You can get up a half-hour earlier, eat a high-protein breakfast, and walk for thirty minutes before you go to work. That will energize you mentally and physically for the rest of the day. Do the same after work, especially if you have been on your feet all day. When I was regularly working twelve-hour shifts—without sitting once during the day—the first thing I did when getting home was to jump on the treadmill for thirty minutes to get the blood moving out of my legs.

Is all that walking too much time and trouble? If you can see yourself fitting easily into your same size jeans in thirty days, is it worth it? It is, absolutely. If you take action when you have just a small weight gain, you will never have to endure the misery of fighting obesity.

Please read the following that I found on a discussion board about exercise and the angst of aging. You may relate to it:

"Those of us between 45 and 65 are not considered seniors—and yet many of us are not comfortable in gyms…We are truly a neglected group. Our local park districts have several senior exercise programs, even senior sports leagues. But we are too young to join them. At the same time, most of us simply can't compete with the 20 and 30-somethings that populate most exercise classes.

Gyms need to go out of their way to be more welcoming to people who don't fit the young and skinny mold. A big part of making a commitment to fitness is psychological, and when you feel you don't belong, that the atmosphere systematically excludes and ostracizes you because you're not 22 years old or you don't weigh 102, then it's extremely difficult to keep going back…

We 40 and 50-somethings are not quite ready for senior citizenship. We want something more suited to our age than what's found in the typical gym. But be very, very careful—I am NOT elderly, and I won't be marketed to or treated that way. Can we find a middle ground for those of us of middle age?"

The above tells me the following about the writer:

- She finds gyms forbidding
- She understands that part of the commitment to exercise is psychological
- She knows forty- and fifty-somethings are not seniors, however…
- She considers forty to fifty middle aged
- She is adamant about not being considered "elderly"

- She has a group mind-set that affects/controls her thinking and behavior

It is the last item on the list above that merits comment first. Managing the aging process is not a group activity. It's nice to have support, and support helps, but ultimately, it's a do-it-yourself project.

I advise forty and fifty-year-olds who need group support to exercise to forget about finding acceptance in a gym populated by twenty-somethings who don't have an inch of flab on their tight bodies. If you must exercise in a group environment, then toughen up. You are not there to compete; you are there to do your own thing. You are there in response to a commitment you made to yourself, not to a group. Part of the commitment to exercise is indeed psychological. If you have made the commitment, you will do what you have to do, regardless of what others do, or where or how they do it.

About avoiding elderly treatment: you can't control the behavior of others. However, if you don't act elderly, others are less likely to treat you as elderly. Do you whine and complain about things that really don't matter? Do you ask and expect others to do for you what you could do for yourself? Do you think you are entitled to special treatment because of your age? If you do any of those things, you are asking to be treated and classified as elderly. As you get closer to retirement there is a tendency to accept the legitimacy of senior status and all the elderly baggage that goes along with it. Don't buy into it. You are not declining into senior-hood; you are growing into a mature woman, and you don't need any additional clarification or classification of your stage of life. Acceptance of senior status is a stone's throw away from elderly status. We will always have "marketing to the elderly" because that's the traditional outcome of the aging process, and most people as they age will fit into that category. Ignore marketing messages that doesn't apply to you.

About middle age: At forty or fifty, you are NOT middle aged! Remember, in the past century our life span has increased by thirty years. Therefore, it no longer makes sense to categorize yourself according to a model that is no longer relevant. There is a better way to think about the stages of aging, and it is found in Dr. Helen Harkness' book *Don't Stop the Career Clock*. I've mentioned it before, but in case you missed it, here it is again. On page 79, Dr. Harkness gives her contemporary model for aging:

- young adulthood: twenty to forty
- first midlife: forty to sixty
- second midlife: sixty to eighty
- young-old: eighty to ninety
- elderly: ninety and above
- old-old: two to three years to live

Be strong, independent, and committed to managing your aging process. Don't look for excuses not to exercise. Realize that regardless of how much group support you have, no one but you can manage how you age. It is the ultimate do-it-yourself project.

Beyond Planning for the Life You Want

Preparation for the life and lifestyle you want in your mature years is crucial. But it's also important to prepare for curve balls life may toss at you.

In response to an article I wrote about managing the aging process, I received this e-mail:

"Barbara, I think you are 'right on.' When I was teaching high school, I felt young and attractive. Now that I have retired and especially now that I am recently widowed, I feel old, useless, and not wanted. A widow becomes a fifth wheel: never invited into the circle of friends you had when you were a couple. When going to group dinners, singles are placed at tables off by themselves. I am now dealing with both age and being without the love of my life and escort. I go to lunch often with other widows (my age).I work in 3 volunteer organizations but all involve old people. Have just finished reading Art Linkletter's book, *How To Make The Rest Of Your Life The Best Of Your Life.* Many of his suggestions require money and a companion, neither of which I have. HELP. Any other good suggestions?????" signed "Luann"

In summary, Luann's message tells me:

- She's retired
- She's widowed
- She's lonely
- She has no plans for the future
- She wants social interaction but not with "old" people
- She volunteers but it is not fulfilling
- She could use more income

Remember, Luann said: "When I was teaching high school, I felt young and attractive. Now that I have retired and especially now that I am recently widowed, I feel old, useless, and not wanted."

Luann felt young and attractive while working because of association with young and attractive, mentally stimulating co-workers. Their youth and vitality helped to stimulate and support her perception of her own youth and vitality. This shows the importance of maintaining relationships or associations with younger people. Few older people have critical youthful contacts that help them feel and function better.

Since I don't know why she retired, I can't comment on her decision, but I do know this: Luann could have had an exit strategy for life after retirement. Retirement is particularly difficult for those who enjoy using their intellect. It's traumatic to stop doing challenging work you've always enjoyed and begin to live life as a mind-numbing pastime. Your self-worth can go down the drain in a hurry.

While Luann's husband was alive, she did what most women do: she failed to think about what might happen to her if her husband died, and what steps she could take to emotionally survive her loss. Because she relied on a close circle of married friends, after her husband's death she had to deal with the reality of being an "outsider" or, as she put it, a "fifth wheel." To avoid being in that situation, while her husband was alive Luann could have gone back to school or joined organizations that would have put her in contact with people of different ages and circumstances—married, divorced, widowed, young, and old. All boomers and beyond should be planning to thrive independently and happily no matter what happens.

Had Luann done such preplanning, it would have broadened her circle of contacts and friends she could rely on for needed social and emotional support. Because she finds it depressing to be around "old" people much of the time, this strategy would have helped her find the diversity of friends she needed when tragedy struck. Someone in this mix of people might even have been a special someone with whom she could later share her unforeseen widowhood.

What really struck me about Luann's situation is that she doesn't have enough money to do some things she would like to do. I constantly harp about financially strapped retirees volunteering when they should be earning a paycheck, and Luann's situation demonstrates the validity of this position. It is upsetting when I see retirees, mentally and physically able, financially doing without for lack of satisfying employment that would enhance their quality of life. Please don't misunderstand—volunteering is a good thing. It can open doors to paid work and keep you connected to the larger world. It's a satisfying way to help others in need. But I don't think seniors should be expected to volunteer when they need work that pays.

You don't have to become a "fifth wheel." You don't have to be lonely. You don't have to struggle financially after traditional retirement age if you are mentally and physically competent. But you do have to plan for the kind of life you want after life throws you a curveball. Thinking ahead will help mitigate a huge amount of potential grief.

Please read *Setbacks and Losses: You Can Bounce Back in Style*[25] by Dr. Donna Marie Thompson. She assures you that there is life after loss. Also read *Nobody Wants to Talk About It—Baby Boomers Face Grief* [26] by Jane Galbraith, B.Sc.N., R.N.

Prepare for Another Reality

It's not news that the "golden years" of many people, especially women, are often hijacked by family members in need of care. It's not just boomers caring for aging parents; it's aging parents caring for the children of their boomer children who, for whatever reason, do not care for their own children.

As a boomer, at this point in your life, your parents may need you to care for them. As you get on in years, you may find yourself caring for your grandkids.

A lengthy article in the local paper about older women who care for very young children was heartbreaking and thought provoking. One woman at ninety-two gets around on a cane and raises her great-grandchildren. Other women in their seventies with arthritis and other health problems severe enough to require others to care for them try their best to raise typically active youngsters.

The story reinforced the reality that you don't know what life will dish out, so assume life will be tough as you age. That means you cannot live day-to-day and just let life happen. If you do that, life WILL just happen, and your reward will be the usual decline that eventually progresses into dependence.

How well you age is the result of how and what you think, the choices you make, and the amount of just plain gritty determination you have very early in your life. It's knowing in your gut that you don't want to be a burden. It's knowing you want to be strong and healthy, mentally and physically, ready for whatever comes along. You want to be able to take care of yourself and your grandkids if need be, or your spouse or other family member who needs help.

If one day you have to parent your great-grand-kids, it could turn out to be a joy instead of a millstone if you are mentally and physically up to the task. You can be in charge of your circumstances if you make a determined effort to take charge of your aging process while you still have the capacity to do so.

ACCEPT AND VALUE YOUR MOTHER'S GIFTS TO YOU

Make Her Your New Best Friend

One very important thing you need to do now is to make a decision to appreciate your mother and all the good things she has done for you. You may be saying, "Of course I appreciate my mom. She's the greatest." However, many adult children have *something*, real or imagined, that they hold against their well-meaning but imperfect parents. For example, remember when you were a rebellious teenager and you hated your mom when she didn't allow you to hang out with Disgusting Druggy with the peace sign on his dirty T-shirt? Since you are probably a mom yourself now, you understand why your mom did what she did, but you still harbor some resentment, if not about Disgusting Druggy then about something else.

Get over it. The past is gone. Unless your mother locked you in a closet, set you on fire, and did other heinous things to you, don't blame your mother for anything. She undoubtedly had "stuff" in her childhood that may not have been resolved, and unintentionally you may have been the recipient of some of her unresolved "stuff." Don't harbor grudges because they do nothing to punish your mother. Refusing to forgive hurts only you. While it may be difficult or impossible to forget, a verbal expression of forgiveness is essential for your well-being. You don't have to speak your forgiveness in the presence of your mother. Just say it aloud and mean it.

She gave you life, and for that, you owe her appreciation. Had she chosen to snuff you out before you entered this world, you wouldn't be here. What you make of your life, even at this late date, is up to you. Adopt her best qualities and use them to your advantage. Keep in mind that one day your kids will have their own list of grievances against you, so be prepared to forgive them as they will (hopefully) forgive you. If there is something you are aware of that needs mending with your kids, do it now.

Abuse of all kinds exists in many homes. Ask yourself this question: Should parents who abused their children expect their children to be their caretakers when they are old? You have to do what you believe is the right thing to do. But this is certain—the cleaner your record as a parent, the easier it will be for conscientious children to make a decision to care for you if and when needed. What goes around, comes around—eventually.

The quality of your mature years will depend on the quality of your mom's mature years. Whatever you can do to help her stay mentally and physically strong and flexible will pay huge dividends for her, for you, and your family. (Preserving the quality of life of your dad is equally important, and much of what applies to Mom goes for Dad.)

If your mom is now in good health and is open to change, there is a lot you can do to help her stay independent and out of a nursing home down the road. Even if you think she's doing great right now and doesn't need help from you, remember that aging successfully is about preparation and effort. Her condition today is no assurance of what she will be like in five years unless both of you prepare. Granted, preparation is not the be-all and end-all of aging successfully, but it significantly improves chances of a happy life.

As years go by, we get comfortable with our lifestyle and change becomes increasingly difficult, so it's important to start early, while she is still aware that she needs to take an active role in managing her aging process. If she can understand that, your job will be easier, and your rewards (and hers) will be greater.

There are important things you can do:

- If she is not in an exercise program, buy her a membership at a gym. Buy one for yourself if needed, and go together. Maintaining strength is crucial for staying independent. As an alternative to a gym, get her a treadmill and motivate her to use it. If you are not using a treadmill, this is a good time to invest in one and perhaps share the cost.

- Buy her a subscription to a good newsletter that will teach her about nutrition and supplements and encourage her to try to stay healthy. If you do not subscribe to one for yourself, perhaps you could split the cost. A good choice would be Dr. Julian Whitaker's newsletter.[27] He takes a commonsense approach to medicine and wellness. I subscribe to his print newsletter and wouldn't be without it.

- Don't be overly solicitous for her welfare. Let her do for herself what she can and wants to do. For example, if Mom wants to wash windows, telling her "You don't have to do that anymore; I can do it for you" is not helpful. If she wants to get down on her knees and scrub the kitchen floor—that's great. It's good exercise.

- Help her stay mentally sharp and strong. Maintaining cognitive function is critical and, contrary to prevailing wisdom, mental decline is not inevitable. You have to exercise the mind as strenuously as you exercise the body. Crossword puzzles are great—for you, too. If she doesn't know how to use a computer, encourage her to sign up for a class. If she doesn't work but would like to, knowing how to use a computer will help her get a worthwhile temporary job.

- If she is in good shape financially, encourage her to spend money on herself. Help her update her appearance and wardrobe. The better she knows she looks, the happier she will be. If she wants to get a face-lift, more power to her. (Just make sure she does her homework before she decides on a surgeon.)

- Encourage her to keep her teeth in good repair. Good oral health is more than cosmetic; it's a health issue if she has bleeding or infected gums or missing teeth. Bacteria from infected gums circulate all over the body, causing achy joints, headaches, and a host of other complaints seemingly without a cause. If she would like braces on her teeth, encourage her to go for it. The Invisalign process is simple and works wonders. I had braces on my teeth when I was sixty-nine. It was a great decision. I still wear my Invisalign retainers every night. Does she want new veneers or crowns? A nice white smile will take years off her appearance.

- Do not treat your mom as your child. If she says she wants to buy something don't ever tell her, "You don't need it." It's her life, her money, not yours, and the two of you will get along much better when you show respect for her wishes. And, because she is not your child, when there is a difference of opinion, remember you are speaking to an adult, not a teenager in need of chastisement.

- If your father is still in the picture and if she is overly dependent on him and he departs this earth unexpectedly, it will be an unnecessary burden for you and for her if she isn't prepared to stand on her own two feet. Make certain she knows the passwords to all financial accounts and where everything is located. It is essential she knows what he knows. If your father does most of the driving, she should be just as comfortable behind the wheel as he is. If she is not used to driving and suddenly has to drive, it takes time to regain confidence. Now is a good time to purchase a GPS for them.

- If she is alone and finds a significant other, be happy for her and try not to meddle. However, if it is clear the guy is a potential threat to her health, happiness, or pocketbook, you have my permission to meddle. You may not know this, but (giggle giggle) some suave old goats are looking for a nurse or a purse—or both. It's unfortunate that many older women are willing to settle for anything just to have someone in their life. Over the prescription counter, I have heard many sad tales about loneliness, frustration, and competition for barely breathing males in the senior community.

• To be fair, I've heard some great stories about love found late in life. But even some heartwarming stories have a sad ending. I recall a woman in her late seventies who became engaged. As she showed me her ring, glowing with happiness, she gushed, "I can't believe it is possible to feel this way at my age." The light in her eyes was that of a teenager. Not too long after, the engagement was off because she discovered "he wasn't the man I thought he was." Better to find out sooner rather than later!

Depending on your own personal situation, you can think of other things to help your mom live happily in her mature years. Think about it now, and do what you can do that will benefit both of you.

YOU GOT WHAT IT TAKES!

Women who successfully manage their aging process have distinct qualities or characteristics that set them apart from women who don't age well. As an ageless, independent woman in a constant state of growth, the following qualities are essential for maintaining smokin' hotness in your maturity:

- You value your health above all else
- You are a confident, independent thinker
- You are intuitive; you know that all is not known about aging and that "certainties" related to aging can be changed or modified
- You do not fear being different
- You recognize life is finite but live as if it isn't
- You have a "can do" overcoming attitude
- You avoid "default aging"—just letting life happen
- You reject limitation thinking and behaviors
- You take responsibility for lifestyle choices

- You define yourself as "mature"—never as "old" or "senior" or "retired"
- You visualize your future, knowing it drives lifestyle choices
- You exercise authority over your survival and anti-survival instincts
- You know that order and discipline foster growth and achievement
- You eat to live and not live to eat
- You do not live a segregated lifestyle
- You observe how others age and use what you see to improve your own aging process
- You live in a spirit of gratitude for all things, good and bad, knowing that adversity can lead to unexpected benefits
- You are a giver, knowing that the more you give of yourself, the more you get in wonderful, unexpected ways
- You have constant awareness of how you are changing and you manage how you are changing
- You avoid adopting the "old" thinking and behaviors of others
- You do not talk about chronological age or allow awareness of it to influence how you live
- You plan for the future, regardless of age

All of the above seems like a lot to internalize and put into practice, but it's not. Much of it is just common sense. Cut and paste the list and put it where you can read it frequently. Incorporate those characteristics into your thinking and lifestyle to help you create the life you want.

THE ULTIMATE PAYOFF

Claim Your Prize—You Earned It

The payoff for taking seriously what I've shared in these pages is not only do you avoid becoming your mother and not adopt her lifestyle, but you win the ultimate prize: freedom, independence, and all the accompanying priceless benefits that result from living a consistently healthy way of life.

Were you hoping for a sexier prize? When you are in your maturity, there is nothing, absolutely nothing more important or sexier than your freedom and independence. Remember, the life span has increased dramatically. You will undoubtedly have many more years of life than you imagine. If you don't think freedom and independence is a big enough prize, think about what it might be like if you are seventy or eighty; your health is gone, your money has run out and you are dependent on the kindness and decency of others to get through each and every day. It's horrible to contemplate and worse than horrible to experience. Don't assume the government will take care of you. With the future of health care in question, if you become a public burden, you may be considered too expensive to keep alive. Too late, you would realize that freedom and independence are indeed the ultimate prize for taking care of yourself over the years.

The following four kinds of personal freedom are imperative to have when you are in your seventh, eighth, or ninth decade of life. Pay particular attention to the fourth type of freedom:

- Freedom that is the result of optimum health that allows growth and independence. You are not free if you can't take care of yourself. A healthy, independent woman is a smokin' hot woman.

- Freedom to be yourself and live as a younger woman. When you are healthy, independent, and full of vibrant life, what is hotter than that? You are free when you can live where you choose to live and go where you want to go.

- Freedom from financial worry, a result of prudent planning and continuous, balanced, lifelong productivity. A smokin' hot woman has money to burn (if she chooses to). She doesn't rely on a man or anyone else to take care of her.

- Freedom from elder abuse. Smokin' hot women don't allow themselves to become or be perceived as a victim or needy.

Of the above four types of freedom, the one freedom few boomer women think about is freedom from elder abuse. When you are younger and healthy, it's seen as something that only happens to very old, dependent people, and that is generally the case. However, the reality is that freedom from elder abuse is something you start to prepare for when you are still foolish enough to think it can't happen to you.

A disturbing article in the *Los Angeles Times*, November 13, 2005, "When a Family Matter Turns into a Business"[28] presented a horrific account of what life can be like when someone you don't know, never met, and without your knowledge or consent decides to be your legal guardian. This nightmare may not be possible in your state, but it's smart to be aware of a type of abuse you may encounter in your maturity.

The article tells what happened to one eighty-seven-year old woman when her life was taken over by a professional conservator.

The professional conservator business is said to be booming and, for the most part, unregulated in California. Conservators have authority over thousands of vulnerable adults, and no agency licenses conservators or investigates complaints against them, according to the *Times* article.

Conservators allegedly find clients by sponsoring breakfasts at senior centers and networking at legal luncheons. Nursing homes allegedly contact them when patients become a problem. Hospitals allegedly call them when patients have outlasted insurance benefits.

Once a senior falls into the grasp of an unwanted conservator, it is difficult and expensive, even with the help of an attorney, to get rid of him or her, as the eighty-seven-year-old woman in the *Times* article discovered.

WHAT YOU CAN DO

- Now is the time to decide who will control your "golden" years. Make legal arrangements to protect yourself. "That time" is closer than you think. In the blink of an eye, you will be there.

- Take control of your health to the best of your ability so that you stay mentally and physically competent as long as possible. Abusers prey on the frail, dependent, and needy. You don't have to fall into decline just because you are aging.

- Be wary of loving friends and family who unintentionally encourage dependence. When your children start to tell you, "You don't have to do that anymore, we can do it for you"—beware. Allowing others to do for you what you can do for yourself is a slippery slope. Accept help when you really need help and say "no thanks" when you don't need it. It's nice to be catered to. The more unneeded help is accepted, the more it is expected and preferred, eventually leading to a real need for increasing amounts of assistance. Personal freedom is fragile and can be lost without realizing it.

- Avoid the entitlement syndrome that afflicts many who accept "senior" status. I can't recall the number of seniors who have told me, "I've done for others all of my life, now it's time for others to do for me." That's a very dangerous attitude. When you do for others, do it because you really want to do it and don't expect anything in return. An entitlement mentality just begs for the intervention of others who are anxious to "do for you" for a profit, and, in the bargain, perhaps take over your life and your finances.

Try to make certain that regardless of how long you live, you will always have your four types of personal freedom. You can't be smokin' hot without them!

THE "RULES"—A REVIEW

Here is a review of what you have read in these pages. It is in the form of "rules" you need to follow if you want to avoid becoming your mother or living her way of life. It's very little about appearance and a whole lot about lifestyle and what you allow to go on in your head.

- Take care of your health. It is your most important possession. Nothing matters more. Not relationships, friends, family, sex, or money. If you don't have your health, you don't have anything. To get it and keep it, educate yourself about nutrition, dietary supplements, and healthy lifestyle choices. If you take care of yourself early on, and if life doesn't throw a curve ball, options in later life are unlimited. If you have been less than kind to yourself over the years, your body can be incredibly forgiving when you start treating it right at least by age forty.

- Discipline yourself. Seventy percent of the aging process is controllable with proper lifestyle choices. Eating and exercising for a high-energy, feel-good way of life now will keep you in peak condition, smokin' hot, eager, and ready for new future challenges and opportunities. You mother may not have known this, but now you do.

• Have an open mind. Find a traditionally trained physician with expertise in antiaging medicine and nutrition or a naturopath to help you rethink your relationship with food and medicine. An antiaging physician who understands natural hormone replacement therapy, natural insulin management, and dietary supplements will get your body in balance so that you are bursting with energy, feeling great, in control of your weight, and free of diabetes. You will love your life and look forward to the future.

• Visualize your future. Know what you want to be like and what you want your life to be like twenty-five years down the road. Commitment to a compelling vision will influence lifestyle choices you make that will result in exciting, "great life" dividends later on.

• At forty and fifty, women are concerned about work, kids, gray hair, weight gain, health issues, dependent parents, and not enough energy. Learn to identify and manage issues in your life that are important now, but at the same time acknowledge and begin to work on what's important long term. Future planning will assure a second life and a second chance to do what you've always wanted to do. You don't have to walk in your mother's shoes unless you choose to.

- Don't talk about your age. Your value is not in the number of years lived. When others know your exact age, you expose yourself to their biases, perceptions, and expectations for how someone "your age" should conform to their stereotypical ideas. Knowledge of your age influences how others interact with you, and it's not always as you would like. The subtleties of ageist treatment are usually not visible to others, but you know it when you are the recipient. It can be painful. Better to keep them guessing.

- Traditional middle age is no longer middle age, so don't focus on your chronological age or allow your awareness of your chronological age to be factored into decisions about how you live.

- Disconnect or distance yourself from people who invite decline, even unintentionally. Choose friends carefully. You learn how to get old from friends and family who don't know how to manage their aging process. Find healthy, positive, future-oriented, productive role models. They can help you improve or change your life. Two hallmarks of oldness are fear of change and inability to accept new ideas. Associate with younger people as much as possible to see life through fresh, adventurous eyes.

- Engage in rigorous mental management. Stop negative self-talk ("I'm too old to do that," "I'm having a senior moment," "I'm an old broad"). You are what you say you are. Negative self-talk isn't cute or endearing; it damages self-esteem and shuts down motivation for improvement and growth. Challenge ageist comments directed at you, however innocently intended. A birthday card with a "You are over the hill" message isn't clever. Tell the sender of the "greeting" why it's not appropriate even if it's socially accepted and "everybody does it." Denigration of the older years has to stop. Be brave and speak up against it.

- Monitor how you are changing. At forty and fifty, take an inventory of youthful characteristics that you want to keep as long as possible, and then work to maintain and improve what you have. In particular, work to hold on to basic youthful attributes such as good posture and mental and physical strength and flexibility. This is more important than worrying about wrinkles. You can hire someone to erase wrinkles, but you can't hire someone to inhabit your head and make you do what you know you must do. Remember, it's easier to keep what you have than to try to get back what's lost.

- Do not move into an age-segregated community. Don't be fooled by the "active adults" lure. Yes, retirement communities are peaceful and quiet and offer tons of amenities, but combine that with expanses of neatly manicured lawns and it's as depressing as living in a cemetery. Retirement communities are places where old-oriented people go to play and decay. (No offense intended if your mother lives in one of those places and is enjoying life— that's her right. But you don't have to live the way she lives.)

- Your world will narrow significantly after unplanned retirement, so in addition to choosing friends carefully and not segregating yourself in a prison-like, walled, gated and guarded adults-only community, make an effort to expand your world, and continue to grow. Do not subscribe to boomer publications that are more suited for seniors or participate in boomer activities and organizations that are senior oriented.

- Do not retire without having a "life plan" as well as a "financial plan" in place. Unplanned traditional retirement exacerbates decline. Remember, the first couple of years in retirement are like a honeymoon. You get to do all the stuff you wanted to do while you were working. But just as marriage honeymoons don't last, neither do retirement honeymoons, so be prepared. Eventually the real world kicks in, and that's when you start to become a "senior." It's all downhill from there unless you are prepared for the life you really want.

- After you "retire," try to work part time at the work you were doing before retirement as long as possible. Staying productive will help you avoid becoming frail and dependent.[29] Better yet, have a plan in place to start a new productive life that will keep you growing. It is the ultimate insurance that will keep you from becoming your mother.

You have the power to manage your aging process if you follow the above "rules," particularly abiding by the mandate not to give in to stultifying traditional retirement. In your "retirement years," reject the "retirement" and "senior" designations and choose to live in a state of vibrant, unbroken, evolutionary growth and productivity.

Enjoy the thrill of cheating Mother Time and getting to sixty, seventy, and beyond and feeling and functioning as you did twenty-five years earlier. Having a life plan for post retirement life and working your plan will result in an incredible payoff at a time when you need it most. Will you stand out like a sore thumb among your peers? Absolutely. But don't flaunt your youthful vitality to make other women feel insecure, envious, or inadequate. Use your wisdom and skills to help them be the women they would still like to be. The more you give of yourself, the more you get back in exciting ways you cannot begin to imagine.

As a teenager, you believed you would never get old. While you can't stop the passage of time, you can manage what goes on while time passes. You don't have to get "old" as your mother did or live her traditional lifestyle. You can stay just as smokin' hot as you are today. If you are not smokin' hot now because you let yourself go, get to work recapturing your hotness. Start right now to do what you know you gotta do to make your future materialize in the way you want it to unfold. It's exciting and you can definitely make it happen. I've done it, I'm still doing it, and you can do it, too.

Girlfriend, let me hear from you. Please tell me what you are doing to create the future you want. If you need encouragement, I'm here to help. Write to me at author.office@gmail.com.

MOVERS AND SHAKERS OVER SEVENTY—YOU CAN BE ONE, TOO

If you think chronologically "old" people can't be productive, then be motivated by these ageless men and women (especially the women) who are enjoying and using their "retirement" to be of value to others as well as themselves. They confirm that you can have a fulfilling life in your mature years.

Bert Roper, 83
Bert Roper has been an innovator in the citrus industry for more than six decades. Now, the Agriculture Hall of Famer is branching out to other entrepreneurial and environmental ventures.

Lisa Gable, 84
Like millions of women, Lisa Gable was often frustrated by falling bra straps. So, at age 70, she designed a solution and launched an intimate apparel company. Fourteen years later, she's still at the helm and her Strap-

Mate can be found at Nordstrom and other major retailers.

Bob Galvin, 85
Bob Galvin transformed Motorola into a worldwide telecommunications giant and helped usher in the wireless age. Now, at 85, he's searching for a solution to the nation's energy crunch.

Phyllis Apple, 84
Phyllis Apple started a thriving public-relations firm at an age when most people start mulling retirement. Nearly three decades later as CEO, she is still putting in forty-hour workweeks.

Bernard Rothzeid, 82
When he's not jetting off to Africa to oversee an American-style hospital his architecture firm is designing, Bernard is back in New York, sketching, brokering new deals, and meeting with clients.

Iris Rubinfield, 80
She helped her husband build a successful manufacturing company. When he passed away, she took the helm. Nearly three decades later, she's transformed Master Manufacturing into one of America's fastest-growing private companies.

Jeno Paulucci, 89
He has more than seventy companies to his credit, including several major frozen-food brands. And he's get-

ting ready to launch another new venture—an attempt to take on Hot Pockets.

Gertrude Boyle, 85
Gertrude has served as chairman of the board of directors of Columbia Sportswear in Portland, Oregon, since 1970.

Lucille Flint, 74
After retirement, Lucille got her licensed to sell real estate and became exceptionally successful, but had a hankering to go back into teaching and learning more about the marketing on the internet. She has done Webinars in USA, Canada, Australia, Paupa New Guinea, New Zealand and the U.K. Lucille is the originator and formulator of the first full line of botanical and natural products now marketed under the name of Grace Cosmetics.

Darlene Dennis, 74
In response to a difficult experience entertaining a houseguest, Darlene wrote Host or Hostage? A Guide for Surviving House Guests, published by Barthur House. Darlene believes strategies for sidestepping or overcoming handicaps and obstacles are essential for continuing self-development and accomplishment. Details at www.hostorhostage.com.

Harriet Hodgson, 75
Harriet has been a journalist for more than thirty years, author of twenty-seven books and hundreds of Internet/print articles. She currently writes for the Open to

Hope Foundation Website and is a monthly columnist for Caregiving in America magazine. Harriet has shared her experiences on many talk shows, including CBS Radio, and dozens of television stations, including CNN. Her latest book, Writing to Recover: The Journey from Loss and Grief to a New Life and the Writing to Recover Journal, are published by Centering Corporation. Details at harriethodgson.com

Ginnie Siena Bivona, 78
Ginnie is President and founder of Atriad Press, publishing Texas non-fiction with a division specializing in self-publishing, working with each client on a one to one basis. Ginnie 's published works include Notes From A Chameleon, Sort of A Memoir, and The Seductive Chef, A Cookbook & More For Lovers. Details at ginniebivona. com, ginniebivona.blogspot.com, atriadpress.com

Other successful mature movers and shakers: Regis Philbin, 78, Barbara Walters, 80, David Oreck, 85, Art Linkletter, 97—to name just a few!

Contact Barbara Morris
author.office@gmail.com

FREE BONUS BOOKLET

Download a complimentary copy of "Tips, Tools, and Resources for The Second Half of Life": **http://www.PutOldonHold.com/tips.pdf**

Fourteen expert authors give practical and immediately usable advice in bite-size pieces for you and those you care about. These well-tested tools and techniques are sure to get you thinking about what works best for you now and in the future.

Endnotes

1   1. Successful Aging by John Wallis Rowe, M.D., and Robert L. Kahn, page 20.

2   2. Economic & Social Research Council (2008, October 11). Sixties Generation Is Heading For Conventional Old Age. ScienceDaily. Retrieved July 20, 2009, from http://www.sciencedaily.com/releases/2008/10/081009072206.htm.

3   3.See note 2 above.

4   4. "People Entering Their 60s May Have More Disabilities Today Than in Prior Generations," http://www.sciencedaily.com/releases/2009/11/091112162832.htm.

5   5. "Say Goodbye to New Year Resolutions" by Joyce Shafer, http://www.putoldonhold.com/newsletter/nov09.html.

6   6. See note 1 above.

7   7. See note 2 above.

8   8. Sign up for the Put Old on Hold Newsletter at http://www.PutOldonHold.com.

9   9. Supercharged Retirement: Ditch the Rocking Chair, Trash the Remote, and Do What You Love, http://mining-silver.com/products_services/superchargedretirement.php.

10 10. Don't Stop the Career Clock, http://www.career-design.com.

11 11. See note 10 above.

12 12. "Beliefs Imperil Funding," Los Angeles Times, March 14, 2004.

13 13. Aired February 2001.

14 14. See note 1 above.

15 15. "Baby Boomers Still Doing Drugs as Seniors," http://www.palmbeachpost.com/health/baby-boomers-still-doing-drugs-as-seniors-169230.html?printArticle=y.

16 16. "New Study Supports Antioxidant Supplements for Ageing Skin," http://www.nutraingredients.com/content/view/print/263252.

17 17. "Women Sacrifice Food Before Cosmetics," http://www.cosmeticsdesign-europe.com/content/view/print/221577.

18 18. http://www.putoldonhold.com/articles/skin_oct08.html

19 19. "New Study Finds Increased Vitamin Use by the Elderly Could Save Medicare $1.6 Billion." http://www.PutOldonHold.com/lewin.pdf.

20 20. "Med Schools Failing on Nutrition Teaching," http://www.nutraingredients-usa.com/news/ng.asp?n=67000&m=1NIU412&c=nszedopdfzvbmwd.

21 21. "Enjoy Better Health, According To National Study." ScienceDaily. Retrieved October 18, 2009, http://www.sciencedaily.com /releases/2009/10/091013105332.htm.

22 22. http://www.local6.com/news/9283707/detail.
html
23 23.http://www.washingtontimes.com/weblogs/
take-weight/2009/jan/12/diet-soda-doorway-to-
weight-gain/
24 24. http://www.whitakerwellness.com
25 25. "Setbacks and Losses: You Can Bounce Back in
Style," http://www.PutOldonHold.com/articles/
thompson_jan10.html.
26 26. "Nobody Wants to Talk About It—Baby Boomers Face Grief," by Jane Galbraith, B.Sc.N., R.N.,
http://www.PutOldonHold.com/articles/gal-
braith_feb10.html.
27 27. See note 23 above.
28 28. http://www.latimes.com/news/local/la-me-
conserve13nov13,1,7970214.story
29 29. "Volunteering May Prevent the Elderly from Becoming Frail," http://www.sciencedaily.com/releas-
es/2010/01/100108090955.htm.